Composting, Grade 5

What if you could challenge your fifth-grade students to investigate the role of composting in solid waste management? With this volume in the *STEM Road Map Curriculum Series*, you can! *Composting* outlines a journey that will steer your students toward authentic problem solving while grounding them in integrated STEM disciplines. Like the other volumes in the series, this book is designed to meet the growing need to infuse real-world learning into K–12 classrooms.

This interdisciplinary, four-lesson module uses project- and problem-based learning to help students use the engineering design process (EDP) to design and create prototypes of compost systems and build a full-scale composting system for school use. Students will synthesize their learning about biotic and abiotic factors, decomposition, and engineering design as they learn about various types of compost systems, create their own portable compost bins, and create materials for a composting publicity campaign at their school.

To support this goal, students will do the following:

- Identify and explain interdependent relationships in ecosystems

- Compare and contrast several ecosystems

- Describe how compost systems are designed and constructed and apply this understanding to creating prototypes of various compost systems

- Understand the concept of scale and apply this understanding to create scaled models of compost systems

- Apply their understanding of composting, compost systems, and the EDP to create a full-scale compost system for the school

- Measure various characteristics of compost

The *STEM Road Map Curriculum Series* is anchored in the Next Generation Science Standards, the Common Core State Standards, and the Framework for 21st Century Learning. In-depth and flexible, *Composting* can be used as a whole unit or in part to meet the needs of districts, schools, and teachers who are charting a course toward an integrated STEM approach.

Carla C. Johnson is a Professor of Science Education and Office of Research and Innovation Faculty Research Fellow at North Carolina State University, North Carolina, USA.

Janet B. Walton is a Senior Research Scholar at North Carolina State's College of Education in Raleigh, North Carolina, USA.

Erin E. Peters-Burton is the Donna R. and David E. Sterling Endowed Professor in Science Education at George Mason University in Fairfax, Virginia, USA.

THE STEM ROAD MAP CURRICULUM SERIES

Series editors: Carla C. Johnson, Janet B. Walton, and Erin E. Peters-Burton

Map out a journey that will steer your students toward authentic problem solving as you ground them in integrated STEM disciplines.

Co-published by Routledge and NSTA Press, in partnership with the National Science Teaching Association, this K–12 curriculum series is anchored in the Next Generation Science Standards, the Common Core State Standards, and the Framework for 21st Century Learning. It was developed to meet the growing need to infuse real-world STEM learning into classrooms.

Each book is an in-depth module that uses project- and problem-based learning. First, your students are presented with a challenge. Then, they apply what they learn using science, social studies, English language arts, and mathematics. Engaging and flexible, each volume can be used as a whole unit or in part to meet the needs of districts, schools, and teachers who are charting a course toward an integrated STEM approach.

Modules are available from NSTA Press and Routledge, and organized under the following themes. For an update listing of the volumes in the series, please visit https://www.routledge.com/STEM-Road-Map-Curriculum-Series/book-series/SRM (for titles co-published by Routledge and NSTA Press), or www.nsta.org/book-series/stem-road-map-curriculum (for titles published by NSTA Press).

Co-published by Routledge and NSTA Press:

Optimizing the Human Experience:

- *Our Changing Environment, Grade K: STEM Road Map for Elementary School*
- *Genetically Modified Organisms, Grade 7: STEM Road Map for Middle School*
- *Rebuilding the Natural Environment, Grade 10: STEM Road Map for High School*
- *Mineral Resources, Grade 11: STEM Road Map for High School*

Cause and Effect:

- *Formation of the Earth, Grade 9: STEM Road Map for High School*

Sustainable Systems:

- *Composting, Grade 5: STEM Road Map for Elementary School*
- *Global Population Issues, Grade 7: STEM Road Map for Middle School*
- *The Speed of Green, Grade 8: STEM Road Map for Middle School*
- *Creating Global Bonds, Grade 12: STEM*
- *Road Map for High School*

Published by NSTA Press:

Innovation and Progress:

- *Amusement Park of the Future, Grade 6: STEM Road Map for Elementary School*
- *Transportation in the Future, Grade 3: STEM Road Map for Elementary School*
- *Harnessing Solar Energy, Grade 4: STEM Road Map for Elementary School*
- *Wind Energy, Grade 5: STEM Road Map for Elementary School*

- *Construction Materials, Grade 11: STEM Road Map for High School*

The Represented World:

- *Patterns and the Plant World, Grade 1: STEM Road Map for Elementary School*
- *Investigating Environmental Changes, Grade 2: STEM Road Map for Elementary School*
- *Swing Set Makeover, Grade 3: STEM Road Map for Elementary School*
- *Rainwater Analysis, Grade 5: STEM Road Map for Elementary School*
- *Packaging Design, Grade 6: STEM Road Map for Middle School*
- *Improving Bridge Design, Grade 8: STEM Road Map for Middle School*
- *Radioactivity, Grade 11: STEM Road Map for High School*
- *Car Crashes, Grade 12: STEM Road Map for High School*

Cause and Effect:

- *Physics in Motion, Grade K: STEM Road Map for Elementary School*
- *Influence of Waves, Grade 1: STEM Road Map for Elementary School*
- *Natural Hazards, Grade 2: STEM Road Map for Elementary School*
- *Human Impacts on Our Climate, Grade 6: STEM Road Map for Middle School*
- *The Changing Earth, Grade 8: STEM Road Map for Middle School*
- *Healthy Living, Grade 10: STEM Road Map for High School*

Composting, Grade 5

Grade
5

STEM Road Map for Elementary School

Edited by Carla C. Johnson, Janet B. Walton, and
Erin E. Peters-Burton

Routledge
Taylor & Francis Group

NEW YORK AND LONDON

nsta Press
National Science Teaching Association

Designed cover images: © Getty Images and © Shutterstock

First published 2024
by Routledge
605 Third Avenue, New York, NY 10158

and by Routledge
4 Park Square, Milton Park, Abingdon, Oxon, OX14 4RN

Routledge is an imprint of the Taylor & Francis Group, an informa business

A co-publication with NSTA Press

Library of Congress Cataloging-in-Publication Data
Names: Johnson, Carla C., 1969– editor. | Walton, Janet B., 1968– editor. | Peters-Burton, Erin E., editor.
Title: Composting, grade 5 / edited by Carla C. Johnson, Janet B. Walton, and Erin E. Peters-Burton.
Description: First edition. | New York, NY : Routledge, 2024. | Series: STEM road map for curriculum series | Includes bibliographical references.
Identifiers: LCCN 2023005278 (print) | LCCN 2023005279 (ebook) | ISBN 9781032441603 (hardback) | ISBN 9781032431178 (paperback) | ISBN 9781003370772 (ebook)
Subjects: LCSH: Compost—Juvenile literature. | Food waste—Recycling—Juvenile literature. | Compost—Experiments—Juvenile literature.
Classification: LCC TD796.5 .C596 2024 (print) | LCC TD796.5 (ebook) | DDC 631.8/75—dc23/eng/20230215
LC record available at https://lccn.loc.gov/2023005278
LC ebook record available at https://lccn.loc.gov/2023005279

ISBN: 978-1-032-44160-3 (hbk)
ISBN: 978-1-032-43117-8 (pbk)
ISBN: 978-1-003-37077-2 (ebk)

DOI: 10.4324/9781003370772

Typeset in Palatino LT Std
by Apex CoVantage, LLC

CONTENTS

Part 1: The STEM Road Map: Background, Theory, and Practice

Part 2: Composting: STEM Road Map Module

CONTENTS

4 Composting Lesson Plans 41

*Andrea R. Milner, Vanessa B. Morrison, Janet B. Walton,
Carla C. Johnson, Erin E. Peters Burton*

CONTENTS

ABOUT THE EDITORS AND AUTHORS

Dr. Carla C. Johnson is a Professor of Science Education and Office of Research and Innovation Faculty Research Fellow at NC State University. Dr. Johnson has served (2015–2021) as the director of research and evaluation for the Department of Defense–funded Army Educational Outreach Program (AEOP), a global portfolio of STEM education programs, competitions, and apprenticeships. She has been a leader in STEM education for the past decade, serving as the director of STEM Centers, editor of the *School Science and Mathematics* journal, and lead researcher for the evaluation of Tennessee's Race to the Top–funded STEM portfolio. Dr. Johnson has published over 200 articles, books, book chapters, and curriculum books focused on STEM education.

She is a former science and social studies teacher and was the recipient of the 2013 Outstanding Science Teacher Educator of the Year award from the Association for Science Teacher Education (ASTE), the 2012 Award for Excellence in Integrating Science and Mathematics from the School Science and Mathematics Association (SSMA), the 2014 award for best paper on Implications of Research for Educational Practice from ASTE, and the 2006 Outstanding Early Career Scholar Award from SSMA. Her research focuses on STEM education policy implementation, effective science teaching, and integrated STEM approaches.

Dr. Janet B. Walton is a senior research scholar at NC State's College of Education in Raleigh, North Carolina. Her research focus includes collaboration between schools and community stakeholders for STEM education, problem- and project-based learning pedagogies, online learning, and mixed methods research methodologies. She leverages a background in workforce development along with her experience in curriculum development to bring contextual STEM experiences into the classroom and provide students and educators with innovative resources and curricular materials. She is the former assistant director of evaluation of research and evaluation for the Department of Defense–funded Army Educational Outreach Program (AEOP), a global portfolio of STEM education programs, competitions, and apprenticeships, and specializes in evaluation of STEM programs.

Dr. Erin E. Peters-Burton is the Donna R. and David E. Sterling endowed professor in science education at George Mason University in Fairfax, Virginia. She uses her experiences from 15 years as an engineer and secondary science, engineering, and mathematics teacher to develop research projects that directly inform classroom practice in science and engineering. Her research agenda is based on the idea that all students should build self-awareness of how they learn science and engineering. She works to help students see themselves as "science-minded" and help teachers create classrooms that support student skills to develop scientific knowledge. To accomplish this, she pursues research projects that investigate ways that students and teachers can use self-regulated learning theory in science and engineering, as well as how inclusive STEM schools can help students succeed. She received the Outstanding Science Teacher Educator of the Year award from ASTE in 2016 and a Teacher of Distinction Award and a Scholarly Achievement Award from George Mason University in 2012, and in 2010 she was named University Science Educator of the Year by the Virginia Association of Science Teachers.

Dr. Toni A. May is an associate professor of assessment, research, and statistics in the School of Education at Drexel University in Philadelphia. Dr. May's research concentrates on assessment and evaluation in education, with a focus on K–12 STEM.

Dr. Andrea R. Milner is the vice president and dean of academic affairs and an associate professor in the Teacher Education Department at Adrian College in Adrian, Michigan. A former early childhood and elementary teacher, Dr. Milner researches the effects constructivist classroom contextual factors have on student motivation and learning strategy use.

Dr. Tamara J. Moore is an associate professor of engineering education in the College of Engineering at Purdue University. Dr. Moore's research focuses on defining STEM integration through the use of engineering as the connection and investigating its power for student learning.

Dr. Vanessa B. Morrison is an associate professor in the Teacher Education Department at Adrian College. She is a former early childhood teacher and reading and language arts specialist whose research is focused on learning and teaching within a transdisciplinary framework.

ACKNOWLEDGMENTS

This module was developed as a part of the STEM Road Map project (Carla C. Johnson, principal investigator). The Purdue University College of Education, General Motors, and other sources provided funding for this project.

See www.routledge.com/9781138804234 for more information about *STEM Road Map: A Framework for Integrated STEM Education*.

PART 1

THE STEM ROAD MAP

BACKGROUND, THEORY, AND PRACTICE

OVERVIEW OF THE *STEM ROAD MAP CURRICULUM SERIES*

Carla C. Johnson, Erin E. Peters-Burton, and Tamara J. Moore

The *STEM Road Map Curriculum Series* was conceptualized and developed by a team of STEM educators from across the United States in response to a growing need to infuse real-world learning contexts, delivered through authentic problem-solving pedagogy, into K–12 classrooms. The curriculum series is grounded in integrated STEM, which focuses on the integration of the STEM disciplines – science, technology, engineering, and mathematics – delivered across content areas, incorporating the Framework for 21st Century Learning along with grade-level-appropriate academic standards. The curriculum series begins in kindergarten, with a five-week instructional sequence that introduces students to the STEM themes and gives them grade-level-appropriate topics and real-world challenges or problems to solve. The series uses project-based and problem-based learning, presenting students with the problem or challenge during the first lesson, and then teaching them science, social studies, English language arts, mathematics, and other content, as they apply what they learn to the challenge or problem at hand.

Authentic assessment and differentiation are embedded throughout the modules. Each *STEM Road Map Curriculum Series* module has a lead discipline, which may be science, social studies, English language arts, or mathematics. All disciplines are integrated into each module, along with ties to engineering. Another key component is the use of STEM Research Notebooks to allow students to track their own learning progress. The modules are designed with a scaffolded approach, with increasingly complex concepts and skills introduced as students progress through grade levels.

The developers of this work view the curriculum as a resource that is intended to be used either as a whole or in part to meet the needs of districts, schools, and teachers who are implementing an integrated STEM approach. A variety of implementation formats are possible, from using one stand-alone module at a given grade level to using all five modules to provide 25 weeks of instruction. Also, within each grade band (K–2, 3–5, 6–8, 9–12), the modules can be sequenced in various ways to suit specific needs.

DOI: 10.4324/9781003370772-2

STANDARDS-BASED APPROACH

The *STEM Road Map Curriculum Series* is anchored in the *Next Generation Science Standards (NGSS)*, the *Common Core State Standards for Mathematics (CCSS Mathematics)*, the *Common Core State Standards for English Language Arts (CCSS ELA)*, and the Framework for 21st Century Learning. Each module includes a detailed curriculum map that incorporates the associated standards from the particular area correlated to lesson plans. The STEM Road Map has very clear and strong connections to these academic standards, and each of the grade-level topics was derived from the mapping of the standards to ensure alignment among topics, challenges or problems, and the required academic standards for students. Therefore, the curriculum series takes a standards-based approach and is designed to provide authentic contexts for application of required knowledge and skills.

THEMES IN THE *STEM ROAD MAP CURRICULUM SERIES*

The K–12 STEM Road Map is organized around five real-world STEM themes that were generated through an examination of the big ideas and challenges for society included in STEM standards and those that are persistent dilemmas for current and future generations:

- Cause and Effect
- Innovation and Progress
- The Represented World
- Sustainable Systems
- Optimizing the Human Experience

These themes are designed as springboards for launching students into an exploration of real-world learning situated within big ideas. Most important, the five STEM Road Map themes serve as a framework for scaffolding STEM learning across the K–12 continuum.

The themes are distributed across the STEM disciplines so that they represent the big ideas in science (Cause and Effect; Sustainable Systems), technology (Innovation and Progress; Optimizing the Human Experience), engineering (Innovation and Progress; Sustainable Systems; Optimizing the Human Experience), and mathematics (The Represented World), as well as concepts and challenges in social studies and 21st century skills that are also excellent contexts for learning in English language arts. The process of developing themes began with the clustering of the *NGSS* performance expectations and the National Academy of Engineering's grand challenges for engineering, which led to the development of the challenge in each module and connections of the module activities to the *CCSS Mathematics* and *CCSS ELA* standards. We performed these mapping processes with large teams of experts and found that these five themes provided breadth, depth, and coherence to frame a high-quality STEM learning experience from kindergarten through 12th grade.

Cause and Effect

The concept of cause and effect is a powerful and pervasive notion in the STEM fields. It is the foundation of understanding how and why things happen as they do. Humans spend considerable effort and resources trying to understand the causes and effects of natural and designed phenomena to gain better control over events and the environment and to be prepared to react appropriately. Equipped with the knowledge of a specific cause-and-effect relationship, we can lead better lives or contribute to the community by altering the cause, leading to a different effect. For example, if a person recognizes that irresponsible energy consumption leads to global climate change, that person can act to remedy his or her contribution to the situation. Although cause and effect is a core idea in the STEM fields, it can actually be difficult to determine. Students should be capable of understanding not only when evidence points to cause and effect but also when evidence points to relationships but not direct causality. The major goal of education is to foster students to be empowered, analytic thinkers, capable of thinking through complex processes to make important decisions. Understanding causality, as well as when it cannot be determined, will help students become better consumers, global citizens, and community members.

Innovation and Progress

One of the most important factors in determining whether humans will have a positive future is innovation. Innovation is the driving force behind progress, which helps create possibilities that did not exist before. Innovation and progress are creative entities, but in the STEM fields, they are anchored by evidence and logic, and they use established concepts to move the STEM fields forward. In creating something new, students must consider what is already known in the STEM fields and apply this knowledge appropriately. When we innovate, we create value that was not there previously and create new conditions and possibilities for even more innovations. Students should consider how their innovations might affect progress and use their STEM thinking to change current human burdens to benefits. For example, if we develop more efficient cars that use by-products from another manufacturing industry, such as food processing, then we have used waste productively and reduced the need for the waste to be hauled away, an indirect benefit of the innovation.

The Represented World

When we communicate about the world we live in, how the world works, and how we can meet the needs of humans, sometimes we can use the actual phenomena to

explain a concept. Sometimes, however, the concept is too big, too slow, too small, too fast, or too complex for us to explain using the actual phenomena, and we must use a representation or a model to help communicate the important features. We need representations and models such as graphs, tables, mathematical expressions, and diagrams because it makes our thinking visible. For example, when examining geologic time, we cannot actually observe the passage of such large chunks of time, so we create a timeline or a model that uses a proportional scale to visually illustrate how much time has passed for different eras. Another example may be something too complex for students at a particular grade level, such as explaining the *p* subshell orbitals of electrons to fifth graders. Instead, we use the Bohr model, which more closely represents the orbiting of planets and is accessible to fifth graders.

When we create models, they are helpful because they point out the most important features of a phenomenon. We also create representations of the world with mathematical functions, which help us change parameters to suit the situation. Creating representations of a phenomenon engages students because they are able to identify the important features of that phenomenon and communicate them directly. But because models are estimates of a phenomenon, they leave out some of the details, so it is important for students to evaluate their usefulness as well as their shortcomings.

Sustainable Systems

From an engineering perspective, the term *system* refers to the use of "concepts of component need, component interaction, systems interaction, and feedback. The interaction of subcomponents to produce a functional system is a common lens used by all engineering disciplines for understanding, analysis, and design" (Koehler et al., 2013, p. 8). Systems can be either open (e.g., an ecosystem) or closed (e.g., a car battery). Ideally, a system should be sustainable, able to maintain equilibrium without much energy from outside the structure. Looking at a garden, we see flowers blooming, weeds sprouting, insects buzzing, and various forms of life living within its boundaries. This is an example of an ecosystem, a collection of living organisms that survive together, functioning as a system. The interaction of the organisms within the system and the influences of the environment (e.g., water, sunlight) can maintain the system for a period of time, thus demonstrating its ability to endure. Sustainability is a desirable feature of a system because it allows for existence of the entity in the long term.

In the STEM Road Map project, we identified different standards that we consider to be oriented toward systems that students should know and understand in the K–12 setting. These include ecosystems, the rock cycle, Earth processes (such as erosion, tectonics, ocean currents, weather phenomena), Earth-Sun-Moon cycles, heat transfer, and the interaction among the geosphere, biosphere, hydrosphere, and atmosphere. Students and teachers should understand that we live in a world of systems that

are not independent of each other, but rather are intrinsically linked such that a disruption in one part of a system will have reverberating effects on other parts of the system.

Optimizing the Human Experience

Science, technology, engineering, and mathematics as disciplines have the capacity to continuously improve the ways humans live, interact, and find meaning in the world, thus working to optimize the human experience. This idea has two components: being more suited to our environment and being more fully human. For example, the progression of STEM ideas can help humans create solutions to complex problems, such as improving ways to access water sources, designing energy sources with minimal impact on our environment, developing new ways of communication and expression, and building efficient shelters. STEM ideas can also provide access to the secrets and wonders of nature. Learning in STEM requires students to think logically and systematically, which is a way of knowing the world that is markedly different from knowing the world as an artist. When students can employ various ways of knowing and understand when it is appropriate to use a different way of knowing or integrate ways of knowing, they are fully experiencing the best of what it is to be human. The problem-based learning scenarios provided in the STEM Road Map help students develop ways of thinking like STEM professionals as they ask questions and design solutions. They learn to optimize the human experience by innovating improvements in the designed world in which they live.

THE NEED FOR AN INTEGRATED STEM APPROACH

At a basic level, STEM stands for science, technology, engineering, and mathematics. Over the past decade, however, STEM has evolved to have a much broader scope and implications. Now, educators and policy makers refer to STEM as not only a concentrated area for investing in the future of the United States and other nations but also as a domain and mechanism for educational reform.

The good intentions of the recent decade-plus of focus on accountability and increased testing has resulted in significant decreases not only in instructional time for teaching science and social studies but also in the flexibility of teachers to promote authentic, problem-solving–focused classroom environments. The shift has had a detrimental impact on student acquisition of vitally important skills, which many refer to as 21st century skills, and often the ability of students to "think." Further, schooling has become increasingly siloed into compartments of mathematics, science, English language arts, and social studies, lacking any of the connections that are overwhelmingly present in the real world around children. Students have experienced school as content provided in boxes that must be memorized, devoid of any real-world context, and often have little understanding of why they are learning these things.

STEM-focused projects, curriculum, activities, and schools have emerged as a means to address these challenges. However, most of these efforts have continued to focus on the individual STEM disciplines (predominantly science and engineering) through more STEM classes and after-school programs in a "STEM-enhanced" approach (Breiner et al., 2012). But in traditional and STEM-enhanced approaches, there is little to no focus on other disciplines that are integral to the context of STEM in the real world. Integrated STEM education, on the other hand, infuses the learning of important STEM content and concepts with a much-needed emphasis on 21st century skills and a problem- and project-based pedagogy that more closely mirrors the real-world setting for society's challenges. It incorporates social studies, English language arts, and the arts as pivotal and necessary (Johnson, 2013; Rennie et al., 2012; Roehrig et al., 2012).

FRAMEWORK FOR STEM INTEGRATION IN THE CLASSROOM

The *STEM Road Map Curriculum Series* is grounded in the Framework for STEM Integration in the Classroom as conceptualized by Moore, Guzey, and Brown (2014) and Moore et al. (2014). The framework has six elements, described in the context of how they are used in the *STEM Road Map Curriculum Series* as follows:

1. The STEM Road Map contexts are meaningful to students and provide motivation to engage with the content. Together, these allow students to have different ways to enter into the challenge.

2. The STEM Road Map modules include engineering design that allows students to design technologies (i.e., products that are part of the designed world) for a compelling purpose.

3. The STEM Road Map modules provide students with the opportunities to learn from failure and redesign based on the lessons learned.

4. The STEM Road Map modules include standards-based disciplinary content as the learning objectives.

5. The STEM Road Map modules include student-centered pedagogies that allow students to grapple with the content, tie their ideas to the context, and learn to think for themselves as they deepen their conceptual knowledge.

6. The STEM Road Map modules emphasize 21st century skills and, in particular, highlight communication and teamwork.

All of the STEM Road Map modules incorporate these six elements; however, the level of emphasis on each of these elements varies based on the challenge or problem in each module.

THE NEED FOR THE *STEM ROAD MAP CURRICULUM SERIES*

As focus is increasing on integrated STEM, and additional schools and programs decide to move their curriculum and instruction in this direction, there is a need for high-quality, research-based curriculum designed with integrated STEM at the core. Several good resources are available to help teachers infuse engineering or more STEM-enhanced approaches, but no curriculum exists that spans K–12 with an integrated STEM focus. The next chapter provides detailed information about the specific pedagogy, instructional strategies, and learning theory on which the *STEM Road Map Curriculum Series* is grounded.

REFERENCES

Breiner, J., Harkness, M., Johnson, C. C., & Koehler, C. (2012). What is STEM? A discussion about conceptions of STEM in education and partnerships. *School Science and Mathematics, 112*(1), 3–11.

Johnson, C. C. (2013). Conceptualizing integrated STEM education: Editorial. *School Science and Mathematics, 113*(8), 367–368.

Koehler, C. M., Bloom, M. A., & Binns, I. C. (2013). Lights, camera, action: Developing a methodology to document mainstream films' portrayal of nature of science and scientific inquiry. *Electronic Journal of Science Education, 17*(2), 1–21.

Moore, T. J., Guzey, S. S., & Brown, A. (2014). Greenhouse design to increase habitable land: An engineering unit. *Science Scope, 37*(7), 51–57.

Moore, T. J., Stohlmann, M. S., Wang, H.-H., Tank, K. M., Glancy, A. W., & Roehrig, G. H. (2014). Implementation and integration of engineering in K–12 STEM education. In S. Purzer, J. Strobel, & M. Cardella (Eds.), *Engineering in pre-college settings: Synthesizing research, policy, and practices* (pp. 35–60). Purdue Press.

Rennie, L., Venville, G., & Wallace, J. (2012). *Integrating science, technology, engineering, and mathematics: Issues, reflections, and ways forward.* Routledge.

Roehrig, G. H., Moore, T. J., Wang, H. H., & Park, M. S. (2012). Is adding the E enough? Investigating the impact of K–12 engineering standards on the implementation of STEM integration. *School Science and Mathematics, 112*(1), 31–44.

STRATEGIES USED IN THE *STEM ROAD MAP CURRICULUM SERIES*

Erin E. Peters-Burton, Carla C. Johnson, Toni A. May, and Tamara J. Moore

The *STEM Road Map Curriculum Series* uses what has been identified through research as best-practice pedagogy, including embedded formative assessment strategies throughout each module. This chapter briefly describes the key strategies that are employed in the series.

PROJECT- AND PROBLEM-BASED LEARNING

Each module in the *STEM Road Map Curriculum Series* uses either project-based learning or problem-based learning to drive the instruction. Project-based learning begins with a driving question to guide student teams in addressing a contextualized local or community problem or issue. The outcome of project-based instruction is a product that is conceptualized, designed, and tested through a series of scaffolded learning experiences (Blumenfeld et al., 1991; Krajcik & Blumenfeld, 2006). Problem-based learning is often grounded in a fictitious scenario, challenge, or problem (Barell, 2006; Lambros, 2004). On the first day of instruction within the unit, student teams are provided with the context of the problem. Teams work through a series of activities and use open-ended research to develop their potential solution to the problem or challenge, which need not be a tangible product (Johnson, 2003).

ENGINEERING DESIGN PROCESS

The *STEM Road Map Curriculum Series* uses engineering design as a way to facilitate integrated STEM within the modules. The engineering design process (EDP) is depicted in Figure 2.1 (p. 10). It highlights two major aspects of engineering design – problem scoping and solution generation – and six specific components of working

DOI: 10.4324/9781003370772-3

Figure 2.1. Engineering Design Process

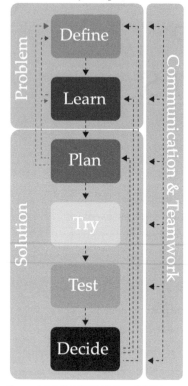

Engineering Design Process
A way to improve

toward a design: define the problem, learn about the problem, plan a solution, try the solution, test the solution, decide whether the solution is good enough. It also shows that communication and teamwork are involved throughout the entire process. As the arrows in the figure indicate, the order in which the components of engineering design are addressed depends on what becomes needed as designers progress through the EDP. Designers must communicate and work in teams throughout the process. The EDP is iterative, meaning that components of the process can be repeated as needed until the design is good enough to present to the client as a potential solution to the problem.

Problem scoping is the process of gathering and analyzing information to deeply understand the engineering design problem. It includes defining the problem and learning about the problem. Defining the problem includes identifying the problem, the client, and the end user of the design. The client is the person (or people) who hired the designers to do the work, and the end user is the person (or people) who will use the final design. The designers must also identify the criteria and the constraints of the problem. The criteria are the things the client wants from the solution, and the constraints are the things that limit the possible solutions. The designers must spend significant time learning about the problem, which can include activities such as the following:

- Reading informational texts and researching about relevant concepts or contexts

- Identifying and learning about needed mathematical and scientific skills, knowledge, and tools

- Learning about things done previously to solve similar problems

- Experimenting with possible materials that could be used in the design

Problem scoping also allows designers to consider how to measure the success of the design in addressing specific criteria and staying within the constraints over multiple iterations of solution generation.

Solution generation includes planning a solution, trying the solution, testing the solution, and deciding whether the solution is good enough. Planning the solution includes generating many design ideas that both address the criteria and meet the constraints.

Here the designers must consider what was learned about the problem during problem scoping. Design plans include clear communication of design ideas through media such as notebooks, blueprints, schematics, or storyboards. They also include details about the design, such as measurements, materials, colors, costs of materials, instructions for how things fit together, and sets of directions. Making the decision about which design idea to move forward involves considering the trade-offs of each design idea.

Once a clear design plan is in place, the designers must try the solution. Trying the solution includes developing a prototype (a testable model) based on the plan generated. The prototype might be something physical or a process to accomplish a goal. This component of design requires that the designers consider the risk involved in implementing the design. The prototype developed must be tested. Testing the solution includes conducting fair tests that verify whether the plan is a solution that is good enough to meet the client and end user needs and wants. Data need to be collected about the results of the tests of the prototype, and these data should be used to make evidence-based decisions regarding the design choices made in the plan. Here, the designers must again consider the criteria and constraints for the problem.

Using the data gathered from the testing, the designers must decide whether the solution is good enough to meet the client and end user needs and wants by assessment based on the criteria and constraints. Here, the designers must justify or reject design decisions based on the background research gathered while learning about the problem and on the evidence gathered during the testing of the solution. The designers must now decide whether to present the current solution to the client as a possibility or to do more iterations of design on the solution. If they decide that improvements need to be made to the solution, the designers must decide if there is more that needs to be understood about the problem, client, or end user; if another design idea should be tried; or if more planning needs to be conducted on the same design. One way or another, more work needs to be done.

Throughout the process of designing a solution to meet a client's needs and wants, designers work in teams and must communicate to each other, the client, and likely the end user. Teamwork is important in engineering design because multiple perspectives and differing skills and knowledge are valuable when working to solve problems. Communication is key to the success of the designed solution. Designers must communicate their ideas clearly using many different representations, such as text in an engineering notebook, diagrams, flowcharts, technical briefs, or memos to the client.

LEARNING CYCLE

The same format for the learning cycle is used in all grade levels throughout the STEM Road Map, so that students engage in a variety of activities to learn about phenomena in the modules thoroughly and have consistent experiences in the problem- and project- based learning modules. Expectations for learning by younger students are

not as high as for older students, but the format of the progression of learning is the same. Students who have learned with curriculum from the STEM Road Map in early grades know what to expect in later grades. The learning cycle consists of five parts – Introductory Activity/Engagement, Activity/Exploration, Explanation, Elaboration/ Application of Knowledge, and Evaluation/Assessment – and is based on the empirically tested 5E model from BSCS (Bybee et al., 2006).

In the Introductory Activity/Engagement phase, teachers introduce the module challenge and use a unique approach designed to pique students' curiosity. This phase gets students to start thinking about what they already know about the topic and begin wondering about key ideas. The Introductory Activity/Engagement phase positions students to be confident about what they are about to learn, because they have prior knowledge, and clues them into what they don't yet know.

In the Activity/Exploration phase, the teacher sets up activities in which students experience a deeper look at the topics that were introduced earlier. Students engage in the activities and generate new questions or consider possibilities using preliminary investigations. Students work independently, in small groups, and in whole-group settings to conduct investigations, resulting in common experiences about the topic and skills involved in the real-world activities. Teachers can assess students' development of concepts and skills based on the common experiences during this phase.

During the Explanation phase, teachers direct students' attention to concepts they need to understand and skills they need to possess to accomplish the challenge. Students participate in activities to demonstrate their knowledge and skills to this point, and teachers can pinpoint gaps in student knowledge during this phase.

In the Elaboration/Application of Knowledge phase, teachers present students with activities that engage in higher-order thinking to create depth and breadth of student knowledge, while connecting ideas across topics within and across STEM. Students apply what they have learned thus far in the module to a new context or elaborate on what they have learned about the topic to a deeper level of detail.

In the last phase, Evaluation/Assessment, teachers give students summative feedback on their knowledge and skills as demonstrated through the challenge. This is not the only point of assessment (as discussed in the section on Embedded Formative Assessments), but it is an assessment of the culmination of the knowledge and skills for the module. Students demonstrate their cognitive growth at this point and reflect on how far they have come since the beginning of the module. The challenges are designed to be multidimensional in the ways students must collaborate and communicate their new knowledge.

STEM RESEARCH NOTEBOOK

One of the main components of the *STEM Road Map Curriculum Series* is the STEM Research Notebook, a place for students to capture their ideas, questions, observations, reflections, evidence of progress, and other items associated with their daily work. At the beginning of each module, the teacher walks students through the setup of the STEM Research Notebook, which could be a three-ring binder, composition book, or spiral notebook. You may wish to have students create divided sections so that they can easily access work from various disciplines during the module. Electronic notebooks kept on student devices are also acceptable and encouraged. Students will develop their own table of contents and create chapters in the notebook for each module.

Each lesson in the *STEM Road Map Curriculum Series* includes one or more prompts that are designed for inclusion in the STEM Research Notebook and appear as questions or statements that the teacher assigns to students. These prompts require students to apply what they have learned across the lesson to solve the big problem or challenge for that module. Each lesson is designed to meaningfully refer students to the larger problem or challenge they have been assigned to solve with their teams. The STEM Research Notebook is designed to be a key formative assessment tool, as students' daily entries provide evidence of what they are learning. The notebook can be used as a mechanism for dialogue between the teacher and students, as well as for peer and self-evaluation.

The use of the STEM Research Notebook is designed to scaffold student notebooking skills across the grade bands in the *STEM Road Map Curriculum Series*. In the early grades, children learn how to organize their daily work in the notebook as a way to collect their products for future reference. In elementary school, students structure their notebooks to integrate background research along with their daily work and lesson prompts. In the upper grades (middle and high school), students expand their use of research and data gathering through team discussions to more closely mirror the work of STEM experts in the real world.

THE ROLE OF ASSESSMENT IN THE *STEM ROAD MAP CURRICULUM SERIES*

Starting in the middle years and continuing into secondary education, the word *assessment* typically brings grades to mind. These grades may take the form of a letter or a percentage, but they typically are used as a representation of a student's content mastery. If well thought out and implemented, however, classroom assessment can offer teachers, parents, and students valuable information about student learning and misconceptions that does not necessarily come in the form of a grade (Popham, 2013).

The *STEM Road Map Curriculum Series* provides a set of assessments for each module. Teachers are encouraged to use assessment information for more than just assigning grades to students. Instead, assessments of activities requiring students to actively engage in their learning, such as student journaling in STEM Research Notebooks, collaborative presentations, and constructing graphic organizers, should be used to move student learning forward. Whereas other curriculum with assessments may include

objective-type (multiple-choice or matching) tests, quizzes, or worksheets, we have intentionally avoided these forms of assessments to better align assessment strategies with teacher instruction and student learning techniques. Since the focus of this book is on project- or problem-based STEM curriculum and instruction that focuses on higher-level thinking skills, appropriate and authentic performance assessments were developed to elicit the most reliable and valid indication of growth in student abilities (Brookhart & Nitko, 2008).

Comprehensive Assessment System

Assessment throughout all STEM Road Map curriculum modules acts as a comprehensive system in which formative and summative assessments work together to provide teachers with high-quality information on student learning. Formative assessment occurs when the teacher finds out formally or informally what a student knows about a smaller, defined concept or skill and provides timely feedback to the student about his or her level of proficiency. Summative assessments occur when students have performed all activities in the module and are given a cumulative performance evaluation in which they demonstrate their growth in learning.

A comprehensive assessment system can be thought of as akin to a sporting event. Formative assessments are the practices: It is important to accomplish them consistently, they provide feedback to help students improve their learning, and making mistakes can be worthwhile if students are given an opportunity to learn from them. Summative assessments are the competitions: Students need to be prepared to perform at the best of their ability. Without multiple opportunities to practice skills along the way through formative assessments, students will not have the best chance of demonstrating growth in abilities through summative assessments (Black & Wiliam, 1998).

Embedded Formative Assessments

Formative assessments in this module serve two main purposes: to provide feedback to students about their learning and to provide important information for the teacher to inform immediate instructional needs. Providing feedback to students is particularly important when conducting problem- or project-based learning because students take on much of the responsibility for learning, and teachers must facilitate student learning in an informed way. For example, if students are required to conduct research for the Activity/Exploration phase but are not familiar with what constitutes a reliable resource, they may develop misconceptions based on poor information. When a teacher monitors this learning through formative assessments and provides specific feedback related to the instructional goals, students are less likely to develop incomplete or incorrect conceptions in their independent investigations. By using formative assessment to detect problems in student learning and then acting on this information, teachers help move student learning forward through these teachable moments.

Formative assessments come in a variety of formats. They can be informal, such as asking students probing questions related to student knowledge or tasks or simply observing students engaged in an activity to gather information about student skills. Formative assessments can also be formal, such as a written quiz or a laboratory practical. Regardless of the type, three key steps must be completed when using formative assessments (Sondergeld et al., 2010). First, the assessment is delivered to students so that teachers can collect data. Next, teachers analyze the data (student responses) to determine student strengths and areas that need additional support. Finally, teachers use the results from information collected to modify lessons and create learning environments that reinforce weak points in student learning. If student learning information is not used to modify instruction, the assessment cannot be considered formative in nature. Formative assessments can be about content, science process skills, or even learning skills. When a formative assessment focuses on content, it assesses student knowledge about the disciplinary core ideas from the *Next Generation Science Standards* (*NGSS*) or content objectives from *Common Core State Standards for Mathematics* (*CCSS Mathematics*) or *Common Core State Standards for English Language Arts* (*CCSS ELA*). Content-focused formative assessments ask students questions about declarative knowledge regarding the concepts they have been learning. Process skills formative assessments examine the extent to which a student can perform science and engineering practices from the *NGSS* or process objectives from *CCSS Mathematics* or *CCSS ELA*, such as constructing an argument. Learning skills can also be assessed formatively by asking students to reflect on the ways they learn best during a module and identify ways they could have learned more.

Assessment Maps

Assessment maps or blueprints can be used to ensure alignment between classroom instruction and assessment. If what students are learning in the classroom is not the same as the content on which they are assessed, the resultant judgment made on student learning will be invalid (Brookhart & Nitko, 2008). Therefore, the issue of instruction and assessment alignment is critical. The assessment map for this book (found in Chapter 3) indicates by lesson whether the assessment should be completed as a group or on an individual basis, identifies the assessment as formative or summative in nature, and aligns the assessment with its corresponding learning objectives.

Note that the module includes far more formative assessments than summative assessments. This is done intentionally to provide students with multiple opportunities to practice their learning of new skills before completing a summative assessment. Note also that formative assessments are used to collect information on only one or two learning objectives at a time so that potential relearning or instructional modifications can focus on smaller and more manageable chunks of information. Conversely,

summative assessments in the module cover many more learning objectives, as they are traditionally used as final markers of student learning. This is not to say that information collected from summative assessments cannot or should not be used formatively. If teachers find that gaps in student learning persist after a summative assessment is completed, it is important to revisit these existing misconceptions or areas of weakness before moving on (Black et al., 2003).

SELF-REGULATED LEARNING THEORY IN THE STEM ROAD MAP MODULES

Many learning theories are compatible with the STEM Road Map modules, such as constructivism, situated cognition, and meaningful learning. However, we feel that the self-regulated learning theory (SRL) aligns most appropriately (Zimmerman, 2000). SRL requires students to understand that thinking needs to be motivated and managed (Ritchhart et al., 2011). The STEM Road Map modules are student centered and are designed to provide students with choices, concrete hands-on experiences, and opportunities to see and make connections, especially across subjects (Eliason & Jenkins, 2012; NAEYC, 2016). Additionally, SRL is compatible with the modules because it fosters a learning environment that supports students' motivation, enables students to become aware of their own learning strategies, and requires reflection on learning while experiencing the module (Peters & Kitsantas, 2010).

The theory behind SRL (see Figure 2.2) explains the different processes that students engage in before, during, and after a learning task. Because SRL is a cyclical learning process, the accomplishment of one cycle develops strategies for the next learning cycle. This cyclic way of learning aligns with the various sections in the STEM Road Map lesson plans on Introductory Activity/Engagement, Activity/ Exploration, Explanation, Elaboration/Application of Knowledge, and Evaluation/Assessment. Since the students engaged in a module take on much of the responsibility for learning, this theory also provides guidance for teachers to keep students on the right track.

Figure 2.2. SRL Theory

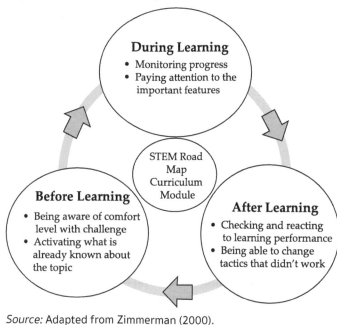

Source: Adapted from Zimmerman (2000).

The remainder of this section explains how SRL theory is embedded within the five sections of each module and points out ways to support students in becoming independent learners of STEM while productively functioning in collaborative teams.

Before Learning: Setting the Stage

Before attempting a learning task such as the STEM Road Map modules, teachers should develop an understanding of their students' level of comfort with the process of accomplishing the learning and determine what they already know about the topic. When students are comfortable with attempting a learning task, they tend to take more risks in learning and as a result achieve deeper learning (Bandura, 1986).

The STEM Road Map curriculum modules are designed to foster excitement from the very beginning. Each module has an Introductory Activity/Engagement section that introduces the overall topic from a unique and exciting perspective, engaging the students to learn more so that they can accomplish the challenge. The Introductory Activity also has a design component that helps teachers assess what students already know about the topic of the module. In addition to the deliberate designs in the lesson plans to support SRL, teachers can support a high level of student comfort with the learning challenge by finding out if students have ever accomplished the same kind of task and, if so, asking them to share what worked well for them.

During Learning: Staying the Course

Some students fear inquiry learning because they aren't sure what to do to be successful (Peters, 2010). However, the STEM Road Map curriculum modules are embedded with tools to help students pay attention to knowledge and skills that are important for the learning task and to check student understanding along the way. One of the most important processes for learning is the ability for learners to monitor their own progress while performing a learning task (Peters, 2012). The modules allow students to monitor their progress with tools such as the STEM Research Notebooks, in which they record what they know and can check whether they have acquired a complete set of knowledge and skills. The STEM Road Map modules support inquiry strategies that include previewing, questioning, predicting, clarifying, observing, discussing, and journaling (Morrison & Milner, 2014). Through the use of technology throughout the modules, inquiry is supported by providing students access to resources and data while enabling them to process information, report the findings, collaborate, and develop 21st century skills.

It is important for teachers to encourage students to have an open mind about alternative solutions and procedures (Milner & Sondergeld, 2015) when working through the STEM Road Map curriculum modules. Novice learners can have difficulty knowing what to pay attention to and tend to treat each possible avenue for information as equal (Benner, 1984). Teachers are the mentors in a classroom and can point out ways

for students to approach learning during the Activity/Exploration, Explanation, and Elaboration/Application of Knowledge portions of the lesson plans to ensure that students pay attention to the important concepts and skills throughout the module. For example, if a student is to demonstrate conceptual awareness of motion when working on roller coaster research, but the student has misconceptions about motion, the teacher can step in and redirect student learning.

After Learning: Knowing What Works

The classroom is a busy place, and it may often seem that there is no time for self-reflection on learning. Although skipping this reflective process may save time in the short term, it reduces the ability to take into account things that worked well and things that didn't so that teaching the module may be improved next time. In the long run, SRL skills are critical for students to become independent learners who can adapt to new situations. By investing the time it takes to teach students SRL skills, teachers can save time later, because students will be able to apply methods and approaches for learning that they have found effective to new situations. In the Evaluation/Assessment portion of the STEM Road Map curriculum modules, as well as in the formative assessments throughout the modules, two processes in the after-learning phase are supported: evaluating one's own performance and accounting for ways to adapt tactics that didn't work well. Students have many opportunities to self-assess in formative assessments, both in groups and individually, using the rubrics provided in the modules.

The designs of the *NGSS* and *CCSS* allow for students to learn in diverse ways, and the STEM Road Map curriculum modules emphasize that students can use a variety of tactics to complete the learning process. For example, students can use STEM Research Notebooks to record what they have learned during the various research activities. Notebook entries might include putting objectives in students' own words, compiling their prior learning on the topic, documenting new learning, providing proof of what they learned, and reflecting on what they felt successful doing and what they felt they still needed to work on. Perhaps students didn't realize that they were supposed to connect what they already knew with what they learned. They could record this and would be prepared in the next learning task to begin connecting prior learning with new learning.

SAFETY IN STEM

Student safety is a primary consideration in all subjects but is an area of particular concern in science, where students may interact with unfamiliar tools and materials that may pose additional safety risks. It is important to implement safety practices within the context of STEM investigations, whether in a classroom laboratory or in the field. When you keep safety in mind as a teacher, you avoid many potential issues with the lesson while also protecting your students.

STEM safety practices encompass things considered in the typical science classroom. Ensure that students are familiar with basic safety considerations, such as wearing protective equipment (e.g., safety glasses or goggles and latex-free gloves) and taking care with sharp objects, and know emergency exit procedures. Teachers should learn beforehand the locations of the safety eyewash, fume hood, fire extinguishers, and emergency shut-off switch in the classroom and how to use them. Also be aware of any school or district safety policies that are in place and apply those that align with the work being conducted in the lesson. It is important to review all safety procedures annually.

STEM investigations should always be supervised. Each lesson in the modules includes teacher guidelines for applicable safety procedures that should be followed. Before each investigation, teachers should go over these safety procedures with the student teams. Some STEM focus areas such as engineering require that students can demonstrate how to properly use equipment in the maker space before the teacher allows them to proceed with the lesson.

Information about classroom science safety, including a safety checklist for science classrooms, general lab safety recommendations, and links to other science safety resources, is available at the Council of State Science Supervisors (CSSS) website at *www.cosss.org/Safety-Resources*. The National Science Teachers Association (NSTA) provides a list of science rules and regulations, including standard operating procedures for lab safety, and a safety acknowledgement form for students and parents or guardians to sign. You can access these resources at *http://static.nsta.org/pdfs/SafetyInThe ScienceClassroom.pdf*. In addition, NSTA's Safety in the Science Classroom web page (*www.nsta.org/safety*) has numerous links to safety resources, including papers written by the NSTA Safety Advisory Board.

Disclaimer: The safety precautions for each activity are based on use of the recommended materials and instructions, legal safety standards, and better professional practices. Using alternative materials or procedures for these activities may jeopardize the level of safety and therefore is at the user's own risk.

REFERENCES

Bandura, A. (1986). *Social foundations of thought and action: A social cognitive theory.* Prentice-Hall.

Barell, J. (2006). *Problem-based learning: An inquiry approach.* Corwin Press.

Benner, P. (1984). *From novice to expert: Excellence and power in clinical nursing practice.* Addison-Wesley Publishing Company.

Black, P., Harrison, C., Lee, C., Marshall, B., & Wiliam, D. (2003). *Assessment for learning: Putting it into practice.* Open University Press.

Black, P., & Wiliam, D. (1998). Inside the black box: Raising standards through classroom assessment. *Phi Delta Kappan, 80*(2), 139–148.

Blumenfeld, P., Soloway, E., Marx, R., Krajcik, J., Guzdial, M., & Palincsar, A. (1991). Motivating project-based learning: Sustaining the doing, supporting learning. *Educational Psychologist, 26*(3), 369–398.

Brookhart, S. M., & Nitko, A. J. (2008). *Assessment and grading in classrooms.* Pearson.

Bybee, R., Taylor, J., Gardner, A., Scotter, P., Carlson, J., Westbrook, A., & Landes, N. (2006). *The BSCS 5E instructional model: Origins and effectiveness.*

Eliason, C. F., & Jenkins, L. T. (2012). *A practical guide to early childhood curriculum* (9th ed.). Merrill.

Johnson, C. (2003). Bioterrorism is real-world science: Inquiry-based simulation mirrors real life. *Science Scope, 27*(3), 19–23.

Krajcik, J., & Blumenfeld, P. (2006). Project-based learning. In R. K. Sawyer (Ed.), *The Cambridge handbook of the learning sciences* (pp. 317–334). Cambridge University Press.

Lambros, A. (2004). *Problem-based learning in middle and high school classrooms: A teacher's guide to implementation.* Corwin Press.

Milner, A. R., & Sondergeld, T. (2015). Gifted urban middle school students: The inquiry continuum and the nature of science. *National Journal of Urban Education and Practice, 8*(3), 442–461.

Morrison, V., & Milner, A. R. (2014). Literacy in support of science: A closer look at cross-curricular instructional practice. *Michigan Reading Journal, 46*(2), 42–56.

National Association for the Education of Young Children (NAEYC). (2016). Developmentally appropriate practice position statements. www.naeyc.org/positionstatements/dap.

Peters, E. E. (2010). Shifting to a student-centered science classroom: An exploration of teacher and student changes in perceptions and practices. *Journal of Science Teacher Education, 21*(3), 329–349.

Peters, E. E. (2012). Developing content knowledge in students through explicit teaching of the nature of science: Influences of goal setting and self-monitoring. *Science and Education, 21*(6), 881–898.

Peters, E. E., & Kitsantas, A. (2010). The effect of nature of science metacognitive prompts on science students' content and nature of science knowledge, metacognition, and self-regulatory efficacy. *School Science and Mathematics, 110*(8), 382–396.

Popham, W. J. (2013). *Classroom assessment: What teachers need to know* (7th ed.). Pearson.

Ritchhart, R., Church, M., & Morrison, K. (2011). *Making thinking visible: How to promote engagement, understanding, and independence for all learners.* Jossey-Bass.

Sondergeld, T. A., Bell, C. A., & Leusner, D. M. (2010). Understanding how teachers engage in formative assessment. *Teaching and Learning, 24*(2), 72–86.

Zimmerman, B. J. (2000). Attaining self-regulation: A social-cognitive perspective. In M. Boekaerts, P. Pintrich, & M. Zeidner (Eds.), *Handbook of self-regulation* (pp. 13–39). Academic Press.

PART 2

COMPOSTING

STEM ROAD MAP MODULE

COMPOSTING MODULE OVERVIEW

Andrea R. Milner, Vanessa B. Morrison, Janet B. Walton,
Carla C. Johnson, and Erin E. Peters-Burton

THEME: Sustainable Systems

LEAD DISCIPLINE: Science

MODULE SUMMARY

In this module, students will investigate the role of composting in solid waste management. Students will learn about biotic and abiotic factors, decomposition, engineering design, and various types of compost systems. They will be challenged to synthesize their learning and use the engineering design process (EDP) to design and create prototypes of compost systems and will also have the option of building a full-scale composting system for school use. Students will also create their own portable compost bins and create materials for a composting publicity campaign at their school (adapted from Capobianco et al., 2015).

ESTABLISHED GOALS AND OBJECTIVES

At the conclusion of this module, students will be able to do the following:

- Identify and explain interdependent relationships in ecosystems

- Compare and contrast several ecosystems

- Describe how compost systems are designed and constructed and apply this understanding to creating prototypes of various compost systems

- Understand the concept of scale and apply this understanding to create scaled models of compost systems

- Apply their understanding of composting, compost systems, and the EDP to create a full-scale compost system for the school

- Measure various characteristics of compost

DOI: 10.4324/9781003370772-5

CHALLENGE OR PROBLEM FOR STUDENTS TO SOLVE: THE COMPOST SYSTEM DESIGN CHALLENGE

Working in teams, students will be challenged to design and build prototypes of composting systems. Each team will research composting systems and design and create a prototype of one type of compost system (i.e., wire-mesh holding unit, turning unit, heap, or worm compost) that could be used by a school cafeteria to turn excess food and food waste into usable compost. An additional option is for the class to build a full-scale composting system appropriate for their school's food waste production.

CONTENT STANDARDS ADDRESSED IN THIS STEM ROAD MAP MODULE

A full listing with descriptions of the standards this module addresses can be found in Appendix B. Listings of the particular standards addressed within lessons are provided in a table for each lesson in Chapter 4.

STEM RESEARCH NOTEBOOK

Each student should maintain a STEM Research Notebook, which will serve as a place for students to organize their work throughout this module (see pp. 12–13 for more general discussion on setup and use of the notebook). All written work in the module should be included in the notebook, including records of students' thoughts and ideas, fictional accounts based on the concepts in the module, and records of student progress through the EDP. The notebooks may be maintained across subject areas, giving students the opportunity to see that although their classes may be separated during the school day, the knowledge they gain is connected. You may also wish to have students include the STEM Research Notebook Guidelines student handout on page 25 in their notebooks.

Emphasize to students the importance of organizing all information in a research notebook. Explain to them that scientists and other researchers maintain detailed research notebooks in their work. These notebooks, which are crucial to researchers' work because they contain critical information and track the researchers' progress, are often considered legal documents for scientists who are pursuing patents or wish to provide proof of their discovery process.

STEM RESEARCH NOTEBOOK GUIDELINES

STEM professionals record their ideas, inventions, experiments, questions, observations, and other work details in notebooks so that they can use these notebooks to help them think about their projects and the problems they are trying to solve. You will each keep a STEM Research Notebook during this module that is like the notebooks that STEM professionals use. In this notebook, you will include all your work and notes about ideas you have. The notebook will help you connect your daily work with the big problem or challenge you are working to solve.

It is important that you organize your notebook entries under the following headings:

1. **Chapter Topic or Title of Problem or Challenge:** You will start a new chapter in your STEM Research Notebook for each new module. This heading is the topic or title of the big problem or challenge that your team is working to solve in this module.

2. **Date and Topic of Lesson Activity for the Day:** Each day, you will begin your daily entry by writing the date and the day's lesson topic at the top of a new page. Write the page number both on the page and in the table of contents.

3. **Information Gathered from Research:** This is information you find from outside resources such as websites or books.

4. **Information Gained from Class or Discussions with Team Members:** This information includes any notes you take in class and notes about things your team discusses. You can include drawings of your ideas here, too.

5. **New Data Collected from Investigations:** This includes data gathered from experiments, investigations, and activities in class.

6. **Documents:** These are handouts and other resources you may receive in class that will help you solve your big problem or challenge. Paste or staple these documents in your STEM Research Notebook for safekeeping and easy access later.

7. **Personal Reflections:** Here, you record your own thoughts and ideas on what you are learning.

8. **Lesson Prompts:** These are questions or statements that your teacher assigns you within each lesson to help you solve your big problem or challenge. You will respond to the prompts in your notebook.

9. **Other Items:** This section includes any other items your teacher gives you or other ideas or questions you may have.

MODULE LAUNCH

Introduce the module topic by showing students a banana peel. Ask students what they would do with the banana peel after they have eaten the banana. Ask them if the banana peel is recyclable and, if they answer affirmatively, how it would be recycled. Next, ask students if they have ever heard of composting. Hold a discussion about what happens to discarded food and options for food waste, and then show a video of how waste is processed at a landfill.

Guide students to understand that there is an alternative to putting food waste into landfills. Introduce the concept that composting is a way to use plant material to create fertilizer that can help other plants grow. Emphasize the concept that composting is a way of recycling food waste.

PREREQUISITE SKILLS FOR THE MODULE

Students enter this module with a wide range of preexisting skills, information, and knowledge. Table 3.1 provides an overview of prerequisite skills and knowledge that students are expected to apply in this module, along with examples of how they apply this knowledge throughout the module. Differentiation strategies are also provided for students who may need additional support in acquiring or applying this knowledge.

Table 3.1. Prerequisite Key Knowledge and Examples of Applications and Differentiation Strategies

Prerequisite Key Knowledge	Application of Knowledge	Differentiation for Students Needing Knowledge
Science		
• Understand cause and and effect relationships.	• Students will understand and describe the role of decomposers and their effects on ecosystems.	• Provide demonstrations and physical models of cause and effect relationships involving the food chain. • Provide a variety of nonfiction literature about the formation of compost and decomposers.
Mathematics		
• Convert numbers from fractions to decimals. • Understand place value of decimal numbers. • Multiply, add, and subtract decimal numbers to thousandths place.	• Students will use mathematics operations when creating tables and graphs for storing and analyzing data.	• Review properties of operations using examples of volume and distance. • Utilize textbook support, teacher instruction, models, graphic organizers, and online instruction to provide practice.

Table 3.1. (*continued*)

Prerequisite Key Knowledge	Application of Knowledge	Differentiation for Students Needing Knowledge
• Understand that measurements expressed as numbers have various units associated with them. • Measure volume and distance with appropriate tools and units. • Make precise measurements.	• Students will make measurements using appropriate units. • Students will make linear measurements and convert them to their decimal equivalents.	• Provide opportunities to practice measuring with precision, using the correct units. • Provide a table that offers a visual reinforcement for measurements and units.
English Language Arts		
• Read grade-level science texts and decode words using phonics and word analysis skills. • Use information gained from illustrations and text to understand science concepts. • Draw inferences from informational text. • Use science terms to write informative texts and explain thoughts and ideas about composting systems. • Provide evidence to support ideas and opinions about topics.	• Students will conduct research about compost systems using the internet and grade-appropriate texts. • Students will read fiction and nonfiction texts that portray topics from the module in a variety of ways. • Students will write informative and explanatory narratives to convey ideas and information, descriptive details, and clear event sequences.	• Provide reading strategies to support comprehension of nonfiction texts, including using vocabulary notecards and games, graphic organizers, STEM Research Notebooks, and discussions. • Through class read-alouds, model interpreting illustrations and graphics in texts and drawing inferences from informational texts. • Provide templates or graphic organizers for writing. • Model organizational techniques for writing. • Provide rubrics for students to assess their own writing.

POTENTIAL STEM MISCONCEPTIONS

Students enter the classroom with a wide variety of prior knowledge and ideas, so it is important to be alert to misconceptions or inappropriate understandings of foundational knowledge. These misconceptions can be classified as one of several types: "preconceived notions," opinions based on popular beliefs or understandings; "nonscientific beliefs," knowledge students have gained about science from sources outside the scientific community; "conceptual misunderstandings," incorrect conceptual

models based on incomplete understanding of concepts; "vernacular misconceptions," misunderstandings of words based on their common use versus their scientific use; and "factual misconceptions," incorrect or imprecise knowledge learned in early life that remains unchallenged (NRC, 1997, p. 28). Misconceptions must be addressed and dismantled in order for students to reconstruct their knowledge, and therefore teachers should be prepared to take the following steps:

- Identify students' misconceptions.
- Provide a forum for students to confront their misconceptions.
- Help students reconstruct and internalize their knowledge, based on scientific models.

(NRC, 1997, p. 29)

Keeley and Harrington (2010) recommend using diagnostic tools such as probes and formative assessment to identify and confront student misconceptions and begin the process of reconstructing student knowledge. Keeley's *Uncovering Student Ideas in Science* series (*www.uncoveringstudentideas.org*) contains probes targeted toward uncovering student misconceptions in a variety of areas and may be useful resources for addressing student misconceptions in this module.

Some commonly held misconceptions specific to lesson content are provided with each lesson so that you can be alert for student misunderstanding of the science concepts presented and used during this module.

SELF-REGULATED LEARNING (SRL) PROCESS COMPONENTS

Table 3.2 illustrates some of the activities in the Composting module and how they align to the SRL processes before, during, and after learning.

Table 3.2. SRL Learning Process Components

Learning Process Components	Example from Composting Module	Lesson Number and Learning Component
Before Learning		
Motivates students	Students discuss what happens to a banana peel after it is removed from the banana and discuss whether it is recyclable.	Lesson 1, Introductory Activity/Engagement
Evokes prior learning	Students discuss composting and answer the questions about their experiences with solid waste.	Lesson 1, Introductory Activity/Engagement

Table 3.2. (*continued*)

Learning Process Components	Example from Composting Module	Lesson Number and Learning Component
During Learning		
Focuses on important features	Students investigate the conditions necessary to maintain composting systems, including the relationship between size of food waste and rate of decay and the results of improper aeration.	Lesson 2, Activity/ Exploration
Helps students monitor their progress	Students track the decomposition of apples sliced in various ways and record data in their STEM Research Notebooks.	Lesson 2, Activity/ Exploration
After Learning		
Evaluates learning	Students create a publicity campaign for composting in the school community that demonstrate their knowledge.	Lesson 4, Elaboration/ Application of Knowledge
Takes account of what worked and what did not work	Students identify problems that could occur with a composting system and how they could be corrected, and reflect on assessment of their work using the presentation rubric.	Lesson 4, Explanation

INTEGRATING INSTRUCTION ACROSS SUBJECTS

The modules of the STEM Road Map take into account that logistics of instruction, such as scheduling and departmentalization, can make teaching integrated subject matter difficult. It is not uncommon, for example, for the same grade-level science and English language arts teachers to have completely different students, which makes integrating science content with content from other subjects difficult. However, we recognize that some schools allow for teachers from different content areas to team teach. The modules of the STEM Road Map Series are written to accommodate both situations – the singular teacher and the teachers who are able to team teach or integrate instruction across subjects in other ways. A teacher who is teaching the module by themselves may choose to follow only the lead subject, offering enrichment activities in the other connecting subjects. Teachers who are teaching the modules in a single subject course may also want to collaborate with their peers in the other disciplinary areas to get ideas for ways to incorporate the supporting connections seamlessly.

Teachers who are able to teach an integrated curriculum can use the module as written for each of the four subjects in the Learning Components sections of the module.

STRATEGIES FOR DIFFERENTIATING INSTRUCTION WITHIN THIS MODULE

For the purposes of this curriculum module, differentiated instruction is conceptualized as a way to tailor instruction – including process, content, and product – to various student needs in your class. A number of differentiation strategies are integrated into lessons across the module. The problem- and project-based learning approaches used in the lessons are designed to address students' multiple intelligences by providing a variety of entry points and methods to investigate the key concepts in the module (for example, investigating composting and recycling using scientific inquiry, fiction and nonfiction literature, journaling, and collaborative design). Differentiation strategies for students needing support in prerequisite knowledge can be found in Table 3.1 (pp. 26–27). You are encouraged to use information gained about student prior knowledge during introductory activities and discussions to inform your instructional differentiation. Strategies incorporated into this lesson include flexible grouping, varied environmental learning contexts, assessments, compacting, tiered assignments and scaffolding, and mentoring.

Flexible Grouping: Students work collaboratively in a variety of activities throughout this module. Grouping strategies you may choose to employ include student-led grouping, placing students in groups according to ability level, grouping students randomly, grouping them so that students in each group have complementary strengths (for instance, one student might be strong in mathematics, another in art, and another in writing), or grouping students according to common interests.

Varied Environmental Learning Contexts: Students have the opportunity to learn in various contexts throughout the module, including alone, in groups, in quiet reading and research-oriented activities, and in active learning in inquiry and design activities. In addition, students learn in a variety of ways through doing inquiry activities, journaling, reading a variety of texts, watching videos, class discussion, and conducting web-based research.

Assessments: Students are assessed in a variety of ways throughout the module, including individual and collaborative formative and summative assessments. Students have the opportunity to produce work via written text, oral and media presentations, and modeling. You may choose to provide students with additional choices of media for their products (for example, PowerPoint presentations, posters, or student-created websites or blogs).

Compacting: Based on student prior knowledge, you may wish to adjust instructional activities for students who exhibit prior mastery of a learning objective. Because student work in science is largely collaborative throughout the module, this strategy may be most appropriate for mathematics, ELA, or social studies activities. You may wish to compile a classroom database of research resources and supplementary readings for a variety of reading levels and on a variety of topics related to the module's topic to provide opportunities for students to undertake independent reading.

Tiered Assignments and Scaffolding: Based on your awareness of student ability, understanding of concepts, and mastery of skills, you may wish to provide students with variations on activities by adding complexity to assignments or providing more or fewer learning supports for activities throughout the module. For instance, some students may need additional support in identifying key search words and phrases for web-based research or may benefit from cloze sentence handouts to enhance vocabulary understanding. Other students may benefit from expanded reading selections and additional reflective writing or from working with manipulatives and other visual representations of mathematical concepts. You may also work with your school librarian to compile a set of topical resources at a variety of reading levels.

Mentoring: As group design teamwork becomes increasingly complex throughout the module, you may wish to have a resource teacher, older student, or parent volunteer work with groups that struggle to stay on task and collaborate effectively.

STRATEGIES FOR ENGLISH LANGUAGE LEARNERS

Students who are developing proficiency in English language skills require additional supports to simultaneously learn academic content and the specialized language associated with specific content areas. WIDA has created a framework for providing support to these students and makes available rubrics and guidance on differentiating instructional materials for multilingual learners (see *www.wida.us*). In particular, multilingual learners may benefit from additional sensory supports such as images, physical modeling, and graphic representations of module content, as well as interactive support through collaborative work. This module incorporates a variety of sensory supports and offers ongoing opportunities for multilingual learners to work collaboratively. The focus on composting affords an opportunity for multilingual learners to share culturally diverse experiences with climate conditions, horticulture, agriculture, and solid waste.

Teachers differentiating instruction for multilingual learners should carefully consider the needs of these students as they introduce and use academic language in various language domains (listening, speaking, reading, and writing) throughout this module. To adequately differentiate instruction for multilingual learners, teachers should have an understanding of the proficiency level of each student. The following five overarching preK–5 WIDA learning standards are relevant to this module:

- Standard 1: Language for Social and Instructional Purposes.

- Standard 2: Language for Language Arts.

- Standard 3: Language for Mathematics.

- Standard 4: Language for Science.

- Standard 5: Language for Social Studies.

SAFETY CONSIDERATIONS FOR THE ACTIVITIES IN THIS MODULE

This module's science component focuses on composting and the role of decomposers in composting. All laboratory occupants must wear safety glasses or goggles during all phases of inquiry activities (setup, hands-on investigation, and takedown) and laboratory floor surfaces must be kept dry to prevent slipping. For more general safety guidelines, see the section on Safety in STEM in Chapter 2 (pp. 18–19) and for lesson-specific safety information, see the Safety Notes section of each lesson in Chapter 4.

DESIRED OUTCOMES AND MONITORING SUCCESS

The desired outcomes for this module are outlined in Table 3.3, along with suggested ways to gather evidence to monitor student success. For more specific details on desired outcomes, see the Established Goals and Objectives sections for the module and individual lessons.

Table 3.3. Desired Outcomes and Evidence of Success in Achieving Identified Outcomes

Desired Outcome	Evidence of Success in Achieving Identified Outcome	
	Performance Tasks	Other Measures
Students will understand and demonstrate their knowledge about the interdependent relationships in ecosystems and the significant role decomposers play within these ecosystems.	• Students will maintain STEM Research Notebooks that will contain graphic organizers with data from investigations, sketches, research notes, evidence of collaboration, and related work from all disciplinary areas. • Students will use their school cafeteria as a design lab to plan a composting system. • Students will be able to defend their design decisions. • Students will be assessed using rubrics that focus on learning and application of skills related to the academic content.	• STEM Research Notebooks will be assessed using a STEM Research Notebook rubric. • Student collaboration will be evaluated using self-assessment reflections, peer feedback, and a collaboration rubric.

ASSESSMENT PLAN OVERVIEW AND MAP

Table 3.4 provides an overview of the major group and individual *products* and *deliverables*, or things that comprise the assessment for this module. See Table 3.5 for a full assessment map of formative and summative assessments in this module.

Table 3.4. Major Products/Deliverables in Lead Discipline for Groups and Individuals

Lesson	Major Group Products/ Deliverables	Major Individual Products/ Deliverables
1	• Ecosystems from Ecosystem Engineers activity • Ecosystem Showcase presentations	• Schoolyard Ecosystem biotic and abiotic factors list • STEM Research Notebook entries
2	• Composting Containers research • Composting Containers presentation	• Gas It Up activity data sheet • Composting Containers paper • STEM Research Notebook entries
3	• Composting system prototypes • Composting system presentations • Composting system budgets • Composting publicity campaign materials	• Measure It diagrams • Prototype It graphic organizers • STEM Research Notebook entries
4	• Class composting system • Class public relations campaign • Maintenance schedule • Data collection plan • Troubleshooting guide research	• STEM Research Notebook entries

Table 3.5. Assessment Map for Composting Module

Lesson	Assessment	Group/ Individual	Formative/ Summative	Lesson Objective Assessed (students will:)
1	STEM Research Notebook *prompts*	Individual	Formative	• Describe the characteristics of an ecosystem. • Identify several interdependent relationships and their effects within ecosystems. • Identify and describe biotic and abiotic components of ecosystems. • Define what a decomposer is and describe the effects of decomposers on ecosystems. • Compare and contrast several ecosystems.

Continued

Table 3.5. (*continued*)

Lesson	Assessment	Group/ Individual	Formative/ Summative	Lesson Objective Assessed (students will:)
1	Ecosystem Engineers *activity handouts*	Group	Formative	• Apply their understanding of abiotic and biotic factors to creating an ecosystem. • Apply their understanding of the engineering design process (EDP) to solve a problem.
1	Ecosystem Showcase Presentations *rubric*	Group	Formative	• Identify and describe several interdependent relationships and their effects within ecosystems. • Identify and describe biotic and abiotic components of ecosystems.
				• Identify several disadvantages of sending solid waste to landfills and identify and describe recycling as an alternative. • Describe composting as a type of recycling.
2	STEM Research Notebook *prompts*	Individual	Formative	• Predict, observe, and explain the relationship between the size of organic material and the rate of decomposition. • Pose researchable questions and collect data about those questions. • Compare and contrast several ecosystems.
2	Room to Rot activity *handouts*	Group/ Individual	Formative	• Describe microbes as a cause of decomposition and use this understanding to explain their observations of decomposition. • Predict, observe, and explain the relationship between the size of organic material and the rate of decomposition.
2	Gas It Up activity *handouts*	Individual	Formative	• Describe the role of aeration in composting and identify the effects of lack of aeration in compost. • Describe microbes as a cause of decomposition and use this understanding to explain their observations of decomposition.

Lesson	Assessment	Group/ Individual	Formative/ Summative	Lesson Objective Assessed (students will:)
2	Composting Containers *research*	Individual	Formative	• Identify several types of composting systems. • Identify and describe the components of a compost system. • Describe how composting systems are constructed.
2	Composting Containers Presentation *rubric*	Group	Formative	• Identify and describe the components of a composting system. • Describe how composting systems are constructed. • Describe how elements of an ecosystem interact in a composting system. • Describe a composting system and its components in a media presentation.
2	Composting Containers *student written reports*	Individual	Formative	• Identify and describe the components of a composting system. • Describe how composting systems are constructed. • Describe how elements of an ecosystem interact in a composting system. • Describe a composting system in an informative essay.
3	STEM Research Notebook *prompts*	Individual	Formative	• Compare and contrast several ecosystems.
3	Measure It *diagrams*	Group	Formative	• Create scaled drawings of a compost system.
3	Composting System Prototypes *rubric*	Group	Summative	• Apply their understanding of how compost systems are designed and constructed to create a compost system prototype. • Use the EDP to create a compost system prototype.

Continued

Table 3.5. (*continued*)

Lesson	Assessment	Group/ Individual	Formative/ Summative	Lesson Objective Assessed (students will:)
3	Composting Systems *presentation rubrics*	Group	Summative	• Explain important features of their composting system.
3	Composting Systems budgets *handout*	Group	Summative	• Create a budget for a full-scale composting system.
3	Composting Publicity Campaign Materials *performance task*	Group	Summative	• Identify the elements of publicity campaigns and apply these elements to create a campaign for composting at their school.
4	Class Composting System *performance task*	Group	Summative	• Apply their understanding of composting principles and composting systems to create a full-scale composting system for school use.
4	Class public relations campaign *performance task*	Group	Summative	• Identify the elements of publicity campaigns and apply these elements to create a campaign for composting at their school.
4	Maintenance Schedule & Data Collection *plan*	Group	Summative	• Explain how to maintain and sustain the compost systems. • Identify data that can be collected about compost and create a plan to collect those data. • Explain how compost is used in gardening.
4	Troubleshooting Guide	Group	Summative	• Identify potential problems that may arise in a composting system and identify solutions for those problem.

MODULE TIMELINE

Tables 3.6–3.10 (pp. 37–39) provide lesson timelines for each week of the module. The timelines are provided for general guidance only and are based on class times of approximately 45 minutes.

Table 3.6. STEM Road Map Module Schedule Week 1

Day 1	Day 2	Day 3	Day 4	Day 5
Lesson 1 *Ecosystem Explorers* Introduce module with discussion of food waste. Show video about landfills. Introduce module challenge. Students begin "Need to Know" chart for module challenge.	*Lesson 1* *Ecosystem Explorers* Students continue "Need to Know" chart. Show video about how compost is made. Discuss components of compost, ecosystems, and decomposers. Students begin discussing and investigating their school lunch waste.	*Lesson 1* *Ecosystem Explorers* Discuss waste management in local community. Students participate in Schoolyard Ecosystem activity.	*Lesson 1* *Ecosystem Explorers* Students share biotic and abiotic factors identified in Schoolyard Ecosystem activity. Introduce Ecosystem Engineers activity. Introduce EDP.	*Lesson 1* *Ecosystem Explorers* Students conduct Ecosystem Engineers research. Create ecosystems for Ecosystem Engineers.

Table 3.7. STEM Road Map Module Schedule Week 2

Day 6	Day 7	Day 8	Day 9	Day 10
Lesson 1 *Ecosystem Explorers* Students present ecosystems in Ecosystem Showcase. Recycling Tour.	*Lesson 1* *Ecosystem Explorers* Discuss water bottle waste in Flint Michigan and show related videos. Students plan and write a work of fiction about a plastic water bottle.	*Lesson 1* *Ecosystem Explorers* Students create plan to maintain and observe ecosystems. Students investigate recyclable and non-recyclable materials in their school lunches. Students provide feedback for peers' fictional work.	*Lesson 2* *Composting Systems* Class discussion of soil fertility. Read aloud *Compost It* by David Barker. Class discussion of benefits and requirements of composting.	*Lesson 2* *Composting Systems* Begin Room to Rot activity (ongoing observations for remainder of module). Introduce Gas It Up activity with discussion of decomposers. Students begin Gas It Up (make observations over next 7 classes).

Table 3.8. STEM Road Map Module Schedule Week 3

Day 11	Day 12	Day 13	Day 14	Day 15
Lesson 2 *Composting Systems* Begin Water Weight activity. Optional field trip.	*Lesson 2* *Composting Systems* Gas It Up activity (ongoing observations for about 7 days). Water Weight activity.	*Lesson 2* *Composting Systems* Begin Composting. Containers research.	*Lesson 2* *Composting Systems* Make observation for Room to Rot activity. Finish Composting Containers research; create presentations and student essays.	*Lesson 2* *Composting Systems* Composting Containers presentations. Peer review of student composting system essays.

Table 3.9. STEM Road Map Module Schedule Week 4

Day 16	Day 17	Day 18	Day 19	Day 20
Lesson 3 Prototyping Compost Systems Read *Rotten Pumpkin* by David Schwartz. Identify biotic and abiotic factors in the rotting pumpkin described in the story; compare and contrast a rotting pumpkin with a compost heap. Introduce budgeting.	*Lesson 3 Prototyping Compost Systems* Introduce publicity campaign. Show video "How to Use Compost." Measure It activity (preparation for prototype). Read *Perimeter, Area, and Volume: A Monster Book of Dimensions* by David Adler.	*Lesson 3 Prototyping Compost Systems* Prototype It activity.	*Lesson 3 Prototyping Compost Systems* Make observation for Room to Rot activity. Complete Prototype It activity. Create compost system budgets. Create printed materials for compost publicity campaign.	*Lesson 3 Prototyping Compost Systems* Teams present prototypes and budgets. Wonderful Worms activity.

Table 3.10. STEM Road Map Module Schedule Week 5

Day 21	Day 22	Day 23	Day 24	Day 25
Lesson 4 The Compost System Design Challenge Students discuss uses of compost and create plan for compost use. Begin building compost system. Post composting campaign materials.	*Lesson 4 The Compost System Design Challenge* Begin Build It activity (building full-scale composting system).	*Lesson 4 The Compost System Design Challenge* Continue building compost system. Create maintenance schedule and data collection plan.	*Lesson 4 The Compost System Design Challenge* Make observation for Room to Rot activity. Continue building compost system. Conduct troubleshooting guide research and create troubleshooting guide.	*Lesson 4 The Compost System Design Challenge* Finish building compost system. Complete troubleshooting guide.

RESOURCES

The media specialist can help teachers locate resources for students to view and read about composting, solid waste, decomposers, and related content. Special educators and reading specialists can help find supplemental sources for students needing extra support in reading and writing. Additional resources may be found online. Community resources for this module may include soil scientists, biologists, local compost center operators, local recycling center operators, and local landfill workers.

REFERENCES

Capobianco, B. M., Parker, C., Laurier, A., & Rankin, J. (2015). The STEM road map for grades 3–5. In C. C. Johnson, E. E. Peters-Burton, & T. J. Moore (Eds.), *STEM Road Map: A framework for integrated STEM education* (pp. 68–95). Routledge. *www.routledge.com/products/9781138804234.*

Keeley, P., & Harrington, R. (2010). *Uncovering student ideas in physical science* (Vol. 1). NSTA Press.

National Research Council (NRC). (1997). *Science teaching reconsidered: A handbook.* National Academies Press.

WIDA. (2020). *WIDA English language development standards framework, 2020 edition: Kindergarten–grade 12.* Board of Regents of the University of Wisconsin System. *https://wida.wisc.edu/sites/default/files/resource/WIDA-ELD-Standards-Framework-2020.pdf.*

COMPOSTING LESSON PLANS

Andrea R. Milner, Vanessa B. Morrison, Janet B. Walton,
Carla C. Johnson, Erin E. Peters Burton

Lesson Plan 1:
Ecosystem Explorers

This lesson will introduce students to composting as a type of recycling. Students will consider implications of society's production of solid waste and the effects of recycling of all types on solid waste management and ecosystem health. In this lesson, students will explore the concept of interdependence in ecosystems with a focus on the interaction of biotic and abiotic factors. Students will create a variety of ecosystems for continued observation throughout the module.

ESSENTIAL QUESTIONS

- What is an ecosystem?

- How do interdependent relationships affect ecosystems?

- What does it mean to say that an ecosystem is sustainable?

- What is a decomposer?

- What are abiotic factors in an ecosystem?

- What are biotic factors in an ecosystem?

ESTABLISHED GOALS AND OBJECTIVES

At the conclusion of this lesson, students will be able to do the following:

- Describe the characteristics of an ecosystem

- Identify and describe several interdependent relationships and their effects within ecosystems

- Identify biotic and abiotic components of ecosystems

DOI: 10.4324/9781003370772-6

- Define what a decomposer is and describe the effects of decomposers on ecosystems

- Identify several disadvantages of sending solid waste to landfills and identify and describe recycling as an alternative

- Describe composting as a type of recycling

- Apply their understanding of abiotic and biotic factors to creating an ecosystem

- Apply their understanding of the engineering design process (EDP) to solve a problem

TIME REQUIRED

8 days (approximately 45 minutes each day; see Tables 3.6–3.7, pp. 37–38)

MATERIALS

Required Materials for Lesson 1

- STEM Research Notebooks (for each student)

- Internet access

- *Bag in the Wind* by Ted Kooser

- Chart paper

- Markers

- Banana peel

Additional Materials for Ecosystems Engineers (1 per team [either teams of 3–4 students or 4 teams per class – see Preparation for Lesson 1, pp. 52–53])

Ant Farm Team

- Scissors

- 1 empty clear plastic 1 liter bottle with lid

- 1 empty clear plastic 2 liter bottle with lid

- Garden soil – about 4 cups

- Duct tape

- Ants – about 30 live Red Harvester ants (available from, for example, *www.antsalive.com/buy-live-ants.htm*)

- Food for ant farm (for example, tiny scraps of fruit waste, bread crumbs)

Aquarium Team

- Small aquarium tank (3–5 gallons) and supplies as recommended by tank manufacturer
- 1–2 fish well-suited for small aquariums (for example, Least Killifish, Norman's Lampeye Killifish; see *www.buildyouraquarium.com/small-freshwater-fish/* for more suggestions)
- Aquarium plants
- Water to fill tank
- Chemical additive to remove chlorine from water

Venus Flytrap Team

- Scissors
- 1 empty clear plastic 2 liter bottle
- 3 cups of garden soil
- Venus flytrap (for information on where to purchase, see *www.flytrapcare.com/where-to-buy-venus-fly-traps-how-expensive/*)

Worm Farm Team

- 1 empty clear plastic 2 liter bottle
- 4 cups of sand
- 4 cups of garden soil
- Small scraps of non-citrus fruit waste (for example, banana and apple peels)
- About 12 worms such as *Eisenia foetida* and *Lumbricus rubellis*, also known as red worms, red wigglers, tiger worms, or manure worms (available from a local bait shop or online; see *www.gardeningchannel.com/where-to-find-composting-worms/* for suggestions)

Additional Materials for Mathematics Connection (1 per team of 3–4 students)

- Scale (to record weight in grams)
- Several types of empty containers to weigh (empty lunch box, a freezer pack, an empty water bottle, several empty Ziploc bags, empty juice box, etc.)

SAFETY NOTES

1. Remind students that personal protective equipment (safety glasses or goggles, aprons, and gloves) must be worn during the setup, hands-on, and take-down segments of activities.

2. Caution students not to eat any materials used in activities.

3. Students should use caution when handling scissors as the sharp points and blades can cut or puncture skin.

4. Tell students to be careful when handling containers. Cans and cut plastic may have sharp edges, which can cut or puncture skin. Glass or plastic bottles can break and cut skin.

5. Immediately wipe up any spilled water or soil on the floor to avoid a slip-and-fall hazard.

6. Instruct students to be aware of and avoid poisonous plants and insects, any refuse, sharps (broken glass), and other hazards when they are outdoors.

7. Have students wash hands with soap and water after activities are completed.

CONTENT STANDARDS AND KEY VOCABULARY

Table 4.1 lists the content standards from the *Next Generation Science Standards* (*NGSS*), *Common Core State Standards* (*CCSS*), and the Framework for 21st Century Learning that this lesson addresses, and Table 4.2 (p. 47) presents the key vocabulary. Vocabulary terms are provided for both teacher and student use. Teachers may choose to introduce some or all of the terms to students.

Table 4.1. Content Standards Addressed in STEM Road Map Module
Lesson 1

NEXT GENERATION SCIENCE STANDARDS

PERFORMANCE OBJECTIVES

- 5-ESS2–1. Develop a model using an example to describe ways the geosphere, biosphere, hydrosphere, and/or atmosphere interact.
- 5-ESS3–1. Obtain and combine information about ways individual communities use science ideas to protect the Earth's resources and environment.
- 5-LS2–1. Develop a model to describe the movement of matter among plants, animals, decomposers, and the environment.

DISCIPLINARY CORE IDEAS

ESS3.C: Human Impacts on Earth Systems
- Human activities in agriculture, industry, and everyday life have had major effects on the land, vegetation, streams, ocean, air, and even outer space. But individuals and communities are doing things to help protect Earth's resources and environment.

ETS1.A: Defining and Delimiting Engineering Problems
- Possible solutions to a problem are limited by available materials and resources (constraints). The success of a designed solution is determined by considering the desired features of a solution (criteria). Different proposals for solutions can be compared on the basis of how well each one meets the specified criteria for success or how well each takes the constraints into account.

ETS1.C: Optimizing the Design Solution
- Different solutions need to be tested in order to determine which of them best solves the problem, given criteria and the constraints.

CROSSCUTTING CONCEPTS

Systems and System Models
- A system is a group of related parts that make up a whole and can carry out functions its individual parts cannot.
- A system can be described in terms of its components and their interactions.

Cause and Effect
- Events have causes that generate observable patterns.
- Simple tests can be designed to gather evidence to support or refute student ideas about causes.

Influence of Science, Engineering, and Technology on Society and the Natural World
- People's needs and wants change over time, as do their demands for new and improved technologies.
- Engineers improve existing technologies or develop new ones to increase their benefits, decrease known risks, and meet societal demands.

SCIENCE AND ENGINEERING PRACTICES

Planning and Carrying Out Investigations
- Plan and conduct an investigation collaboratively to produce data to serve as the basis for evidence, using fair tests in which variables are controlled and the number of trials considered.
- Evaluate appropriate methods and/or tools for collecting data.
- Make observations and/or measurements to produce data to serve as the basis for evidence for an explanation of a phenomenon or test a design solution.
- Make predictions about what would happen if a variable changes.
- Test two different models of the same proposed object, tool, or process to determine which better meets criteria for success.

Continued

Table 4.1. (*continued*)

Obtaining, Evaluating, and Communicating Information
- Read and comprehend grade-appropriate complex texts and/or other reliable media to summarize and obtain scientific and technical ideas and describe how they are supported by evidence.
- Compare and/or combine across complex texts and/or other reliable media to support the engagement in other scientific and/or engineering practices.
- Combine information in written text with that contained in corresponding tables, diagrams, and/or charts to support the engagement in other scientific and/or engineering practices.
- Obtain and combine information from books and/or other reliable media to explain phenomena or solutions to a design problem.
- Communicate scientific and/or technical information orally and/or in written formats, including various forms of media as well as tables, diagrams, and charts.

COMMON CORE STATE STANDARDS FOR MATHEMATICS

MATHEMATICAL PRACTICES
- 5.MP1. Make sense of problems and persevere in solving them.
- 5.MP2. Reason abstractly and quantitatively.
- 5.MP3. Construct viable arguments and critique the reasoning of others.
- 5.MP4. Model with mathematics.
- 5.MP5. Use appropriate tools strategically.
- 5.MP6. Attend to precision.
- 5.MP7. Look for and make use of structure.
- 5.MP8. Look for and express regularity in repeated reasoning.

MATHEMATICAL CONTENT
- 5.MD.A.1. Convert among different-sized standard measurement units within a given measurement system (for example, convert 5 cm to 0.05 m), and use these conversions in solving multi-step, real world problems.

COMMON CORE STATE STANDARDS FOR ENGLISH LANGUAGE ARTS

READING STANDARDS
- RI.5.4. Determine the meaning of general academic and domain-specific words and phrases in a text relevant to a grade 5 topic or subject area.
- RI.5.7. Draw on information from multiple print or digital sources, demonstrating the ability to locate an answer to a question quickly or to solve a problem efficiently.
- RI.5.9. Integrate information from several texts on the same topic in order to write or speak about the subject knowledgeably.

WRITING STANDARDS
- W.5.2. Write informative/explanatory texts to examine a topic and convey ideas and information clearly.
- W.5.4. Produce clear and coherent writing in which the development and organization are appropriate to task, purpose, and audience.

SPEAKING AND LISTENING STANDARDS
- SL.5.1. Engage effectively in a range of collaborative discussions (one-on-one, in groups, and teacher-led) with diverse partners on grade 5 topics and texts, building on others' ideas and expressing their own clearly.

FRAMEWORK FOR 21ST CENTURY LEARNING
- Interdisciplinary themes (financial, economic, & business literacy; environmental literacy)
- Learning and Innovation Skills
- Information, Media & Technology Skills
- Life and Career Skills

Table 4.2. Key Vocabulary in Lesson 1

Key Vocabulary	Definition
abiotic	non-living things
bacteria	microscopic living things that can cause organic material to decay
biotic	describes living things
compost	decayed plant material that is used as a nutrient to enrich soil
decay	the process of bacteria and fungi working together to gradually break down organic material
decomposer	an organism that breaks down organic material
decomposition	the process of gradual decay
earthworm	a tube-shaped worm that lives in soil and whose movement through the soil aerates it
ecosystem	a community of living things interacting with non-living things and their environment
fungi	a kind of organism that feeds on and helps to break down organic material
interdependent	describes how two or more organisms depend on one another for a basic need
landfill	an area of land that contains layers of garbage buried underground
nitrogen	a chemical element found in food waste
nutrient	material in food that provides the energy for living things to grow
nutrient cycle	a process of natural recycling in which nutrients move from the environment to living organisms and then back to the environment
organic	a term used to describe something that is part of a living thing
organism	a living thing such as a person, animal, plant, or bacteria
temperature	a measure of the heat in a substance that can be measured by a thermometer

TEACHER BACKGROUND INFORMATION
Composting

This module focuses on small-scale, low-technology composting as a way of recycling food waste. Composting is an example of a nutrient cycle in which natural materials move between the atmosphere, the soil, and living organisms. In this lesson, students will create systems that allow them to observe the nutrient cycle in plant and animal habitats over time. These observations will serve as a means to understand the interactions that occur during composting. For more information about the nutrient cycle, see the EarthHow "Nutrient Cycle" webpage at *https://earthhow.com/nutrient-cycle/*.

Compost is essentially a mix of a variety of organic materials that decompose quickly because of the work of microbes in an environment where oxygen is available (aerobic). These aerobic microbes speed up the process of decomposition and can turn organic waste into fertile soil that can be used as topsoil, as mulch, or to amend soils. An efficient compost system will have similar amounts of "brown" (leaves, newspaper, napkins, sawdust) and "green" (fruit scraps, vegetable scraps, egg shells, grass clippings, etc.) materials, although compost with more green material will decompose more quickly. Adding some soil from a forest or other microbe-rich environment will help to accelerate the compost process. Compost also needs a moderate amount of water (comparable to a wet sponge) and must be mixed to ensure that oxygen is available to the microbes. Compost may have an earthy odor but it should not have a foul smell. Foul odors from compost indicate that the compost may be too wet or that more "brown" content is required. Foods that should not be composted include meats, fish, dairy products, and grease or oils (adding these to compost will cause a nutrient imbalance with the fruit and vegetable 2materials, will create an odor, and may attract rodents and maggots). The following resources about composting may be useful as you and your class make decisions about what type of composting bin to construct for the school:

- *www.lsuagcenter.com/~/media/system/d/7/c/d57c9aceee429cdcfda31aa37a053688/pub2622compost2.pdf*

- *www.udel.edu/academics/colleges/canr/news/2021/september/art-of-composting/*

An option for this module is to create a full-size compost system at your school. As you consider options, you should consult with school administration, cafeteria staff, and custodial staff. Placement and maintenance of the compost system are important issues to address at the outset of this module. Options to discuss with school staff are to either have student teams build one of each of the four types of composting systems or, alternatively, to decide upon one type of composting system that will be most appropriate for the space available and school health and safety considerations. The four types of composting systems are: wire-mesh holding unit, turning unit, compost heap, and worm compost bin. The compost system designs can be scaled up to a large size; however, composting bins of the size to accommodate all school food waste will be expensive to build and will require a great deal of space. For example, four bins, each measuring $4' \times 4' \times 4'$, are required to meet the composting needs of a school that generates 50 pounds per day of food waste, with materials costing in excess of $800 with 72 hours of construction labor time (Coughlin, n.d.). You may find it necessary to adjust your compost system goals, therefore, to align with your resource availability. You may wish, for instance, to pursue smaller-scale options including creating a compost system for your classroom into which students deposit their school lunch waste. The Composting Council provides numerous resources for planning and executing a composting project (*https://hub.compostingcouncil.org*). You may also wish to work with a local recycling organization and/or a local hardware store for support with the compost system construction.

If it is not possible to construct a full-scale composting system at your school, you may wish to investigate whether it is possible to construct a composting system for another local institution such as a community center. If you choose to do this, you should be sure that the organization with which you collaborate is willing to undertake compost maintenance. Alternatively, if it is not possible to construct a full-scale compost system, you may wish to proceed through the end of Lesson 3 of this module, and have students create a proposal for a composting system to be created at your school rather than having them construct the system.

In addition, starting a school compost system requires a waste separation system. This can be as simple as providing a plastic bin in the school cafeteria into which students empty food waste and compostable materials; however, school-wide education and support about this food separation system will be necessary. You may wish to extend this module by having students create a school-wide campaign promoting composting and providing guidance for other students and staff about food separation.

Ecosystems

In this lesson, students will explore the interdependent relationships in ecosystems and the significant role decomposers play as well as the implications of landfills on human vitality. In this lesson, students create several contained ecosystems for observation throughout the module. These habitats incorporate living organisms, and you should review the NSTA Position statement on responsible use of live animals in the classroom at *www.nsta.org/about/positions/animals.aspx*.

STEM Career Connections

The Bureau of Labor Statistics' *Occupational Outlook Handbook* at *www.bls.gov/ooh/home.htm* provides overviews of numerous STEM careers. You may wish to introduce students to the following STEM career connections during this module (Capobianco et al., 2015):

Compost center operator

Ecologist

Environmental scientist

Geographer

Soil scientist

Biologist

Engineer

Engineering Design Process

Students should understand that engineers need to work in groups to accomplish their work, and that collaboration is important for designing solutions to problems. Students will use the EDP, the same process that professional engineers use in their work, in this lesson. A graphic representation of the EDP is provided at the end of this lesson (p. 65). You may wish to provide each student with a copy of the EDP graphic or enlarge it and post it in a prominent place in your classroom for student reference throughout the module. Be prepared to review each step of the EDP with students and emphasize that the process is not a linear one – at any point in the process, they may need to return to a previous step. The steps of the process are as follows:

1. *Define.* Describe the problem you are trying to solve, identify what materials you are able to use, and decide how much time and help you have to solve the problem.

2. *Learn.* Brainstorm solutions and conduct research to learn about the problem you are trying to solve.

3. *Plan.* Plan your work, including making sketches and dividing tasks among team members if necessary.

4. *Try.* Build a device, create a system, or complete a product.

5. *Test.* Now, test your solution. This might be done by conducting a performance test, if you have created a device to accomplish a task, or by asking for feedback from others about their solutions to the same problem.

6. *Decide.* Based on what you found out during the Test step, you can adjust your solution or make changes to your device.

After completing all six steps, students can share their solution or device with others. This represents an additional opportunity to receive feedback and make modifications based on that feedback.

The following are additional resources about the EDP:

- *www.sciencebuddies.org/engineering-design-process/engineering-design-compare-scientific-method.shtml*

- *www.pbslearningmedia.org/resource/phy03.sci.engin.design.desprocess/what-is-the-design-process*

Books

Books that are specifically integrated into lesson plans are included in the lesson materials lists. A list of suggested books for additional reading can be found at the end of this chapter (see p. 144).

COMMON MISCONCEPTIONS

Students will have various types of prior knowledge about the concepts introduced in this lesson. Table 4.3 outlines some common misconceptions students may have concerning these concepts. Because of the breadth of students' experiences, it is not possible to anticipate every misconception that students may bring as they approach this lesson. Incorrect or inaccurate prior understanding of concepts can influence student learning in the future, however, so it is important to be alert to misconceptions such as those presented in the table.

Table 4.3. Common Misconceptions About the Concepts in Lesson 1

Topic	Student Misconception	Explanation
Ecosystems	Ecosystems are a collection of organisms that live in close proximity to one another.	Ecosystems include interactions between various organisms and the interactions between the organisms and their environment.
	Organisms that are higher in a food chain only eat all organisms that are below them in the food chain.	Organisms in a food chain eat some of the organisms below them in the food chain, but not necessarily all of them.
	Species living in an ecosystem co-exist and do not compete for resources.	Species compete for resources within an ecosystem.

PREPARATION FOR LESSON 1

Review the Teacher Background Information provided (pp. 48–51), assemble the materials for the lesson, make copies of the student handouts, and preview the videos recommended in the Learning Plan Components section that follows. Prepare to have your students set up their STEM Research Notebooks (see pp. 24–25 for discussion and a student instruction handout).

The Ecosystem Engineers activity challenges students to work in teams to construct ecosystems and observe these ecosystems over time. If this is cost prohibitive for your classroom, you may wish to work as a class to construct a single ecosystem to observe. These ecosystems will allow students to observe nutrient cycles (natural recycling pathways through which nutrients are consumed, released, and reused in the natural world). You will work as a class to create a simple diagram of a nutrient cycle. You may wish to identify an example to use as a comparison for the diagram the class creates by conducting a Google search using terms such as "nutrient cycle diagram for elementary" (for example, *https://classnotes.ng/lesson/nutrient-cycling-in-nature-biology-ss2/*). As students create their ecosystems and make observations, you should be prepared to discuss with them how they see nutrients being cycled through the ecosystems.

Note that live animals (fish, ants, and worms) are required for this activity. Plan for appropriate storage of the animals prior to their use in the classroom. Teams will each create one ecosystem in this activity. You should plan for teams to create at least one of each of the four ecosystems (ant farm, aquarium, Venus flytrap, and worm farm). You may choose to split the class into four teams, with each team creating one ecosystem or, alternatively, you may wish to split the class into smaller teams of three to four students each. In the latter case, you will likely duplicate some of the ecosystems. Assemble materials for each ecosystem. You may wish to prepare some materials by, for example, cutting and poking holes in plastic bottles in advance (see Ecosystem Engineers activity, pp. 57–59 for more details).

For the social studies connections, identify a local news media story about waste management in your area to use to launch a class discussion. The example of Flint, Michigan's water crisis is used in this lesson to highlight the issue of plastic water bottles as a solid waste issue. You may wish to familiarize yourself with the current quality of and issues surrounding Flint, Michigan water by visiting a website such as that of the Department of Health and Human Services for residents that provides an overview of the water safety issues they face (this can be accessed at *www.phe.gov/emergency/events/Flint/Pages/default.aspx*).

Students will explore the school grounds in the Schoolyard Ecosystem activity in this lesson. Check the weather report and prepare appropriately for this activity. A school recycling tour is incorporated into this lesson as well. Make appropriate preparations for students to walk through various parts of the school (for example, offices, teacher work spaces, cafeteria, kitchen) to identify recycling activities at the school.

LEARNING PLAN COMPONENTS
Introductory Activity/Engagement

Connection to the Challenge: Begin each day of this lesson by directing students' attention to the module challenge, the Compost System Design Challenge. Introduce the challenge by telling students that they will work in teams and that their team will be challenged to research composting systems and design and build a prototype of a composting system for use by a school's cafeteria so that the excess food and food waste that is disposed of each day can be turned into usable compost. If you choose to have the class build a full-scale composting system appropriate for your school's food waste production, tell students about this activity also.

Hold a brief class discussion each day of how students' learning in the previous days' lessons contributed to their ability to complete the challenge. You may wish to create a class list of key ideas on chart paper.

Science Class: Introduce the module topic by showing students a banana peel. Ask students what they would do with the banana peel after they have eaten the banana. Ask them if the banana peel is recyclable and, if they respond affirmatively, how the peel might be recycled. Next, ask students if they have ever heard of composting. Hold a discussion about what happens to discarded food and options for food waste. Hold a discussion about composting by asking questions such as:

- What do you do with your leftover food at home?

- What do you do with your leftover food at school?

- Do you know what your school does with discarded food?

Many students may answer that their leftover food goes into the trash. Follow up by asking students what happens to food and other items that they put into the trash. Show students the landfill image attached at the end of this lesson plan. Ask students if they have ever seen a landfill in person. Ask them to share some descriptive words for landfills (for example, tall, smelly, dirty).

Show students a video about landfills and how garbage is processed such as Pearson Biology "Video Field Trip – Landfill" at *www.youtube.com/watch?v=mA608GJ-EzM*. After the video, ask students what options for solid waste other than landfills they heard about in the video (for example, recycling). Ask students why it might be important to limit the amount of waste that ends up in landfills (for example, space, environmental contamination). Then ask students to brainstorm in groups of three to

four about what types of materials can be recycled and what can't be recycled. After students have brainstormed for about 5 minutes, create a class list for each category and have each group add the recyclable and un-recyclable items they brainstormed to the list.

Ensure that students understand that there is an alternative to putting food waste into landfills. Introduce the concept to students that composting is a way to use plant material to create fertilizer that can help other plants grow. Emphasize that composting is a way of recycling food waste.

Remind students that they will be challenged to design a composting system for their school that will help keep food waste out of landfills and that creates compost that can be used as garden fertilizer. Have students work in groups of three to four to brainstorm a list of what they think they will need to know to address this challenge (for example, what is in compost, what kind of composting systems are there, how are compost systems constructed, how do compost systems need to be maintained, how much food waste is there at the school, will school administration agree to allow composting at the school, what materials are needed?). After groups have brainstormed for 5–10 minutes, have each group share its ideas with the class, creating a class list of ideas.

Have students create a "Need to Know" chart in their STEM Research Notebooks that incorporates the key ideas identified during the "need to know" brainstorming session. This chart should include the concept, a column for students to note their prior knowledge about the concept, and a column for what they learn about the concept throughout the module. The class should revisit and add to this chart at the close of each lesson.

Ask students to share their ideas about how food waste is turned into fertilizer in a compost system (students can record these ideas in the "Need to Know" chart). Show a video about how compost is made, such as the Recycle Now Campaign video "How Compost is Made" found at *www.youtube.com/watch?v=cBkBwVFFEWw*.

After viewing the video, ask students to name the important components of a compost system. Prompt students to include:

- A container

- Green waste

- Brown waste

- Insects

- Decomposers such as worms and bacteria

Point out to students that a community of creatures works together in the compost bin to create the compost. Tell students that this is an example of an ecosystem. Ask students:

- What is an ecosystem? (lead students to an understanding that it is a community of living things interacting with non-living things and their environment and that an ecosystem is a collection of individual habitats that interact in complex ways).

- How did you see living and non-living things interacting in the composting video? (introduce the concept of biotic, or living, components like insects and bacteria and abiotic, or non-living, components like temperature, the container, sunlight, and moisture).

- What is a decomposer? (lead students to an understanding that a decomposer is an organism that feeds on dead plant and animal material and breaks it down into other substances).

Mathematics Connection: Have students estimate the weight of the food waste they produce on an individual level each day. Record student ideas. Ask for three student volunteers who have packed their lunches. Weigh each lunch and record the weight of each lunch. Ask students if this is the true weight of the food. Remind students that the packaging and containers used for the lunches also have weight. Ask students for ideas about how to find the weight of the actual food in the lunch (Total weight – weight of packaging = weight of food). Ask them to estimate how much of the food weight they eat and how much they dispose of each day.

ELA and Social Studies Connection: Share a local news media report about waste management issues in your community. Hold a class discussion in which students identify the topic of the report, the problem being discussed, the evidence provided, and the solutions proposed. Hold a class discussion about how waste is managed in your local area and how waste management may impact the community and people who live there. Next, hold a class discussion about how the report used words and images to convey information effectively, asking students:

- What about this report captured the reader's or viewer's attention?

- How did the report use images? Do these images help the reader or viewer understand the problem? How?

- Did the report include interviews with community members? How did this affect the reader or viewer?

Activity/Exploration

Science Class: Students will explore ecosystems through three activities. First, students will explore the school grounds to identify biotic and abiotic factors in the environment in the Schoolyard Ecosystem activity. Then, they will create four contained ecosystems for ongoing class observation in the Ecosystem Engineers activity. Students will also tour the school to identify types of recycling that occur in the school in the Recycling Tour activity.

Schoolyard Ecosystem

Create a class definition for the terms biotic and abiotic. Have students create a vocabulary section in their STEM Research Notebooks to record these and other new vocabulary terms they encounter throughout the module. Tell students that they are going to explore their schoolyard to find as many biotic and abiotic factors as they can. You may wish to have students work in pairs for this activity. Have students create a Schoolyard Ecosystem page in their STEM Research Notebooks. Have them create two columns on a notebook page, one labeled "Biotic Factors" and the other labeled "Abiotic Factors."

Take students outside with their STEM Research Notebooks and pencils. Have students search the schoolyard to find as many biotic and abiotic factors as they can to add to the columns. Encourage students to look broadly at the environment (for example, sunshine, air) and very closely (for example, looking closely at the ground to see small insects).

Once students have made their lists, return to the classroom and have students share the biotic and abiotic factors they found. Create a class list on chart paper of the biotic and abiotic factors, listing factors in side-by-side columns. Once the class list is complete, have several students come up one at a time to draw lines between factors that they think interact in the environment and explain how (for example, sunlight and grass – the sun helps grass to grow). Students should come to a realization that nearly all factors on the chart interact with each other in some way.

Next, have students draw lines between abiotic and biotic factors that interact in the lists they made in their STEM Research Notebooks. Have each student choose two pairs of abiotic and biotic factors, create a page heading for each pair in their notebooks, and write two to three sentences about how these factors interact with each other and with the environment around them.

Introduce the idea of nutrient cycles to students by asking students for their ideas about where an animal's food comes from (a squirrel, for example). Encourage students to trace the source of foods to plants. Have the students name what plants need to grow (sunlight, water, and nutrients from the soil). Next, ask students where food goes after it is eaten. Encourage students to consider that some of the food is used as energy and that waste is excreted back into the soil. Work as a class to create a diagram that shows how food that the animal consumes is recycled into the soil and helps to provide nutrients to the plants, creating a cycle of nutrition. Tell students that they are going to create ecosystems in the Ecosystems Engineers activity and that they will observe the nutrient cycle in these ecosystems during the coming weeks.

Ecosystem Engineers

Introduce the activity by telling students that they will work in teams to create a variety of ecosystems that they can observe throughout the coming days. Tell students that each team will be responsible for the maintenance of the ecosystem it creates.

As you prepare for the Ecosystem Engineers investigation, ask your students:

- What are the basic needs of all living things? (air, water, food, shelter [habitat], and sunlight)

- What happens when these basic needs are not met?

- What are some reasons these basic needs may not be met?

Group students in four teams or in teams of three to four (in this case students will create duplicates of some ecosystems). Assign each team one of four ecosystems to create and maintain. The teams will create four ecosystems that are analogous to the types of compost systems students will learn about later in the module:

Team 1: Ant Farm (analogous to Wire-Mesh Holding Unit)

Team 2: Aquarium (analogous to Turning Unit)

Team 3: Venus Flytrap (analogous to Heap)

Team 4: Worm Farm (analogous to Worm Compost)

Be sure that each team has all the supplies they need to build their ecosystem at their table/area along with a set of directions (attached at the end of this lesson plan). Before constructing their ecosystems, students will conduct research about the care and maintenance of the organisms in their ecosystems. Students will use the steps of the engineering design process (EDP) to help them work through this process.

Tell students that they are being challenged to create and maintain an ecosystem that includes living creatures. Introduce students to the idea that engineers are professionals who solve problems by designing and building things and that engineers use a structured process, the EDP, to help them do this. Review the steps of the EDP with students (see Teacher Background Information, pp. 50–51). While some instructions are provided for the actual construction or assembly of teams' ecosystems, there are open-ended elements to the tasks (for instance. investigating what the living organisms in their ecosystems need to survive). The handouts attached at the end of this lesson plan prompt students through each step of the EDP.

Team 1: Ant Farm

Students must first conduct research to discover what sort of food the ants require and how it should be provided to them. This information should be included as part of

their plan for their ecosystem. They should find that a small amount (a few teaspoons) of vegetable or fruit matter on top of the soil along with a few drops of water is adequate for the ants, but that they should remove the food every few days and replace it to avoid mold growing.

Students should use the following basic procedure to build their ant farms:

- Clean a clear 2 liter bottle and 1 liter bottle.

- Cut the top 3–4 inches of the 2 liter bottle off (save this).

- Punch several air holes in the top part of the 2 liter bottle that was removed.

- Place the 1 liter bottle (with its lid on) inside the 2 liter bottle to take up space so the ants will build tunnels and lay eggs close to the outer edge to promote better observation.

- Put soil and ants in the space between the two bottles, leaving an inch of empty space at the top of the bottle to prevent the ants from climbing out.

- Replace the top of the 2 liter bottle and tape on with masking tape or duct tape.

Team 2: Aquarium

Students will need to research what sort of food goldfish require and how often they should be fed. They should also investigate means to keep the tank clean (for instance, adding plants or other living organisms) and the water pH balance. This information should be included as part of the plan for the team's aquatic ecosystem. Students should follow the manufacturer's directions for setting up their aquarium.

Team 3: Venus Flytrap

Students should research what sort of food and other nourishment the Venus flytrap requires (for instance, temperature, amount of sunlight, etc.) and include this as part of their plan for their ecosystem.

Students should follow the following basic procedure to build their Venus flytrap ecosystem:

- Clean the clear 2 liter bottle.

- Cut the bottle in half.

- Poke holes in the bottom of the bottle to allow drainage.

- Fill the bottle bottom with potting soil.

- Plant the Venus flytrap.

- For the "lid," cut multiple 4-inch vertical slots around the bottom portion of the top half of the bottle to allow for airflow. (The lid retains moisture and controls the temperature. The clear plastic allows for observation of root growth.)

- Stagger tucking every other slot in and out between the top and the bottom of the bottle.

- Discard the bottle cap.

Team 4: Worm Farm

Students should research what is required to maintain their Worm Farm and include this as part of their ecosystem plan. For instance, students should investigate what happens to the worms if the farm is placed in direct sunlight and how often moisture should be added to the ecosystem.

Students should follow the following basic procedure to build their Worm Farm:

- Clean the clear 2 liter bottle.

- Cut the top of the bottle off.

- Poke holes and add rocks to the bottom of the bottle to allow drainage.

- Alternate layers of sand and then soil until the layers reach close to the top, adding worms and banana peels within the layers.

- Put the bottle top back on (without the cap) to enable air flow. (The lid retains moisture and controls the temperature. The clear plastic allows for observation.)

- Keep in a cool dark place.

Mathematics Connection: Continue the discussion of school lunch food waste from the Introductory Activity/Engagement section. Be prepared with a scale (to record weight in grams or ounces) and several types of empty containers to weigh (empty lunch box, a freezer pack, an empty water bottle, several empty Ziploc bags, empty juice box, etc.). Have students offer their ideas of what units of measurement would be most appropriate to use for the packaging (grams or ounces). Weigh various types of packaging and use this to estimate the weight of the packaging in the full school lunches student volunteers provide. Weigh the full school lunches and have students use this information and the information about the packaging weight to find the weight of the food in the lunches. Ask the student volunteers to keep all the packaging as well as the food waste in their lunch after they have eaten. Re-weigh the consumed lunches and have students calculate the weight of the remaining food waste.

Next, ask students how they can use this information to find the total amount of food waste in packed lunches in their school. You may wish to incorporate percentages in this activity by counting the number of students who pack their lunches versus those who buy their lunches and calculating a percentage. Have students offer ideas about how they can use this information and the weights of the food waste in the volunteers' lunches to create an estimate of food waste in the school. Point out that the weights of packaging and food waste in the lunches are different. Ask students about which weight they should use in calculations. Introduce the concept of averages and calculate an average weight of food waste and an average weight of packaging (you may wish to extend this activity by calculating the weight of disposable packaging only). Have students use the percentage of lunch packers in their class and the average weight of food waste to calculate daily packed lunch food waste for their class. You may also wish to have students perform calculations for disposable packaging waste in packed lunches. Have students perform the same calculations for the entire school.

For whole-school food waste, ask students if there are units other than grams or ounces that could be used to express the amount of waste. Lead students to understand that for large-scale weight measurements, kilograms or pounds may be more appropriate units to use. Instruct students in procedures to convert grams to kilograms or ounces to pounds and have students express their whole-school food waste findings in kilograms or pounds.

Social Studies and ELA Connections: While the focus of this module is on composting, students should keep in mind that there are other ways to reduce the solid waste that goes to landfills. In the Recycling Tour activity, students will tour the school building to identify where recycling occurs and to identify missed opportunities for recycling.

Recycling Tour

Remind students that we, as humans, are a vital part of our ecosystem and the ways that we interact with our surroundings have far-reaching impacts. Read aloud as a class the book *Bag in the Wind* by Ted Kooser and hold a discussion about how far the bag traveled in the story. Discuss how the story would have been different had the bag been recycled rather than going to a landfill.

Take a recycling tour of the school, looking for evidence of recycling (such as recycling bins) or opportunities for recycling. Create a list of opportunities that students see in and around the school (for instance, providing separate bins in the lunch room for food waste and recyclables).

Continue the class discussion about solid waste management by pointing out that disposing of recyclables can also be difficult. Show a news report about donations of water bottles to Flint, Michigan residents when they faced water contamination (for example, the ABC News report "Local Efforts to Give Flint, MI Water" at *www.you tube.com/watch?v=FhOi_cP7mEA*).

Next, have students read a news story about the solid waste disposal issues with empty water bottles in Flint, Michigan, such as the NBC News story "Flint's Next Issue: What to Do with Empty Water Bottles?" at *www.nbcnews.com/storyline/ flint-water-crisis/flint-s-next-issue-what-do-empty-water-bottles-n505781*. Hold a class discussion about the environmental and societal implications of solid waste.

Next, hold a class discussion about the book *Bag in the Wind* by Ted Kooser. Have students identify the elements of fictional texts in this book (setting, characters, problem, solution). Show students an empty plastic water bottle. Tell them that people use up hundreds of millions of these bottles every year, and they are going to create a story about what might happen to just one of these water bottles if it is not disposed of properly. Distribute the Build Your Own Story graphic organizer attached at the end of the lesson plan to each student. Review the graphic organizer and ask students to identify each element of the story in *Bag in the Wind*. Model filling in the graphic organizer.

Next, tell students that they will use the graphic organizers to plan and then write a story in their STEM Research Notebooks in response to a prompt. Provide students with a copy of the creative writing rubric (see Appendix A). Present students with the following prompt: It is a hot summer day and you are outside in your yard playing soccer with your friends. You grab a plastic water bottle from inside and drink the whole thing, then put it under a tree so that you can grab it later and put it in the recycling bin. After another half hour of the soccer game the sky darkens and you hear thunder in the distance as the wind starts to blow harder. Your friends all run for home and your mom calls for you to come inside right away. You forget all about the water bottle until you are inside, but there is thunder and lightning and strong winds so you can't go out to get it. Write a story about what happens to your water bottle over the next two days.

Explanation

Science Class: Have student teams share their ecosystems in the Ecosystem Showcase activity.

Ecosystem Showcase

After teams have created their ecosystems, they should each prepare a brief presentation for the class explaining how they created their ecosystem and providing information about the living organisms in the ecosystem and how these living organisms will contribute to the nutrient cycle. Students should provide information about how they will care for and feed the organisms in their ecosystem and should identify several abiotic and several biotic features of their ecosystem.

Mathematics Connection: This lesson provides an opportunity to introduce measures of central tendency with an emphasis on means or averages. Ensure that students understand that a mean is a calculated average of a set of numbers. Provide students with opportunities to practice calculating averages. For example, you may wish to have students count the number of pencils each has and then calculate a class average. Introduce the idea that the term "percent" means per one hundred. Students should understand that percentages can also be expressed as decimals and fractions and that it is the decimal form that is typically used in calculations.

ELA Connection: Have students work in pairs to read each other's stories. After each student has read his or her partner's story, have the students complete a Build Your Own Story graphic organizer for the story he or she read. After students have completed graphic organizers identifying the parts of their partners' stories, have students compare these to the author student's original graphic organizer. Have students discuss whether they identified the same elements as the author did and, if not, how their ideas differed.

Social Studies Connection: Have students respond to the following questions in their STEM Research Notebooks:

- Were people right to donate water bottles to Flint, Michigan? Why or why not?

- What other solutions were there to get water to residents?

- What are your suggestions for managing water bottle waste?

Elaboration/Application of Knowledge

Science Class: Student teams should each create a plan to maintain and observe their ecosystems through the course of the module. This involves creating a daily schedule of team members' responsibilities. Additionally, students should create a plan for the ecosystem after the module is over. This may involve having someone take the ecosystem home or, in the case of the worm farm, for example, it may be returning the worms to nature in a shady flower bed outside the school.

Students should first create a labeled diagram that shows the nutrient cycle in the ecosystem they created. Then, students should observe each of the four ecosystems on a regular basis, and record their observations at least once a week, making notes and sketches about what they observe and any changes they observe in their ecosystems over time. To do this, you may wish to have students divide a page of their STEM Research Notebooks into four sections for each observation, labeling each section with an ecosystem name, providing a place to make sketches and take notes.

Revisit the "Need to Know" STEM Research Notebook chart students created at the beginning of this lesson. Review the concepts listed in the chart, adding additional concepts as necessary. Have students work in groups of three to four to record information acquired in this lesson about the concepts. Have each group share the information they recorded with the class, ensuring that students' understanding of concepts is accurate.

Mathematics Connection: Extend the packed school lunch activity by identifying what packaging (non-food) waste in the school lunches is recyclable. Have students calculate an average percent of non-recyclable waste in a packed school lunch by examining several packed lunches and weighing the non-recyclable waste in each. After students have calculated an average, have students determine what, based on the average they calculated, would be the weight of non-recyclable waste per day if each person in the class packed their lunch and then if each person in the school packed school lunches on a daily basis. Then have students calculate totals for the entire school year.

ELA Connection: Have students work in pairs to offer each other feedback about their fictional texts created in this lesson's Activity/Exploration. Reviewing students should provide feedback about whether the story's problem and solution were clear, whether the characters and setting were described adequately, and whether there were enough details provided in the story, as well as identifying spelling and grammar errors, and making any other suggestions they feel appropriate. After students have received feedback, have them each revise their story, incorporating their partner's feedback.

Evaluation/Assessment

Performance Tasks

- Schoolyard Ecosystem biotic and abiotic factors list

- Ecosystems from Ecosystem Engineers activity

- Ecosystem Engineers handouts

- Ecosystem Showcase presentations (see rubric in Appendix A)

- Fictional text (see rubric in Appendix A)

Other Measures

- Teacher observations

- STEM Research Notebook entries

- Student participation in teams

INTERNET RESOURCES

Composting resources

- www.lsuagcenter.com/~/media/system/d/7/c/d57c9aceee429cdcfda31aa 37a053688/pub2622compost2.pdf

- *www.udel.edu/academics/colleges/canr/news/2021/september/art-of-composting/*

- https://hub.compostingcouncil.org

Fish for small aquariums

- *www.buildyouraquarium.com/small-freshwater-fish/*

NSTA Position statement on responsible use of live animals in the classroom

- *www.nsta.org/about/positions/animals.aspx*

Bureau of Labor Statistics' *Occupational Outlook Handbook*

- *www.bls.gov/ooh/home.htm*

Engineering design process

- www.sciencebuddies.org/engineering-design-process/engineering-design-compare-scientific-method.shtml

- *www.pbslearningmedia.org/resource/phy03.sci.engin.design.desprocess/what-is-the-design-process*

Nutrient cycle information: EarthHow, "Nutrient Cycle" webpage

- *https://earthhow.com/nutrient-cycle/*

Overview of water safety issues in Flint, Michigan

- *www.phe.gov/emergency/events/Flint/Pages/default.aspx*

Pearson Biology "Video Field Trip – Landfills"

- *www.youtube.com/watch?v=mA608GJ-EzM*

Recycle Now Campaign video "How Compost is Made"

- *www.youtube.com/watch?v=cBkBwVFFEWw*

ABC News report "Local Efforts to Give Flint, MI Water"

- *www.youtube.com/watch?v=FhOi_cP7mEA*

NBC News story "Flint's Next Issue: What to Do with Empty Water Bottles?"

- *www.nbcnews.com/storyline/flint-water-crisis/flint-s-next-issue-what-do-empty-water-bottles-n505781*

Engineering Design Process
A way to improve

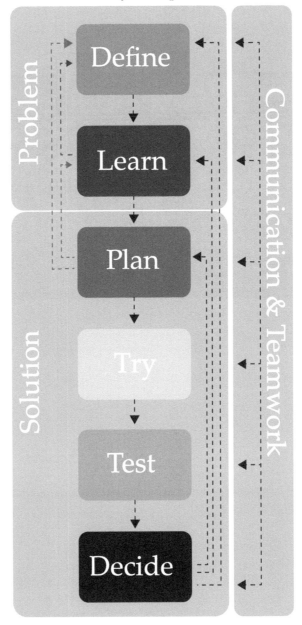

4

Team 1: Ant Farmers
Page 1

Name:_____

Your team will act as farmers – raising ants!

As farmers, you need to create a home for your ants and make sure that their basic needs are met. Use the steps of the EDP to create your ant farm.

Define – What is the problem? _____

Learn: Do some research about your ants!

- What do your ants need to eat? _____

- How will you feed them? _____

- Do they need water? How much? _____

Plan:

- Do you have all the supplies you need to build the farm? _____

- Who will take care of providing the food and water to the ants? You might want to create a schedule for team members to do these jobs.

  _____
  _____
  _____

Look at the building procedure and make a sketch of what your ant farm will look like on the back of this page.

Team 1: Ant Farmers
Page 2

Name:_____

1. **Try.** Use this procedure to build your farm (don't forget to add the food you decided the ants need):

SAFETY NOTE: Always point scissors away from your body and keep hands away from the area in which you are cutting or punching holes.

2. Clean the clear 2 liter bottle and 1 liter bottle.

3. Cut the top 3–4 inches of the 2 liter bottle off (save this) by carefully making a hole with the tip of your scissors where you will begin cutting and then inserting the tip of your scissors in the hole to cut the top off.

4. Punch several air holes in the top part of the 2 liter bottle that was removed using the tip of your scissors.

5. Place the 1 liter bottle (with its lid on) inside the 2 liter bottle to take up space so the ants will build tunnels and lay eggs close to the outer edge to promote better observation.

6. Put soil and ants in the space between the two bottles, leaving an inch of empty space at the top of the bottle to prevent the ants from climbing out.

7. Add the food that your ants need.

8. Replace the top of the 2 liter bottle and tape on with masking tape or duct tape.

Test. Observe your ant farm every day and make notes in your STEM Research Notebook about it.

Decide. After you've observed your ant farm, is there anything that could be improved upon? Is it easy to feed your ants? If not, could you come up with a better system? What other improvements can you think of?

Share. Point out the interesting features of your ant farm to your classmates. If you see the ants doing something interesting, be sure to share that! Explain to your classmates how the design of your farm helps your ants to thrive.

Team 2: Aquatic Action

Page 1

Name:_____

Create an under-the-sea home!

Your job is to create a home for your fish and make sure that their basic needs are met. Use the steps of the EDP to create your aquatic environment.

Define: What is the problem? _____

Learn: Do some research about your fish!

• What do your fish need to eat? _____

• How will you feed them? _____

• What do you need to know about the water you use in the aquarium?

_____
_____

• Do you need to clean the aquarium? How? _____

_____

Team 2: Aquatic Action
Page 2

Name:_____

Plan:

- Do you have all the supplies you need to build the aquatic ecosystem? _____

- Who will take care of feeding the fish and maintaining the aquarium? You might want to create a schedule for team members to do these jobs.

_____

_____

Look at the building procedure and make a sketch of what your aquarium will look like (use the back of this page if you need more space):

Try. Follow the directions that came with the aquarium to build your aquatic ecosystem, or ask your teacher for instructions.

Test. Observe your aquarium every day and make notes in your STEM Research Notebook about it.

Decide. After you've observed your aquatic ecosystem, is there anything that could be improved upon? What improvements can you think of?

Share. Point out the interesting features of your aquarium to your classmates. If you see the fish doing something interesting, be sure to share that! Explain to your classmates how the design of your aquarium helps your fish to thrive.

Team 3: Plant Power
Page 1

Name:_____

This powerful plant needs a home!

Your job is to create an ecosystem for your Venus flytrap and make sure that its basic needs are met. Use the steps of the EDP to create your ecosystem.

Define: What is the problem? _____

Learn: Do some research about your Venus flytrap!

- What does your plant need to eat? _____

- How will you feed it? _____

- How much sunlight does it need? _____

- How much water does it need? _____

Plan:

- Do you have all the supplies you need to build the ecosystem? _____

- Who will take care of caring for your Venus flytrap? You might want to create a schedule for team members to do these jobs.

  _____
  _____
  _____

Look at the building procedure and make a sketch of what your Venus flytrap ecosystem will look like on the back of this page.

Team 3: Plant Power
Page 2

Name:_____

Try. Follow these steps to build your Venus flytrap habitat:

SAFETY NOTE: Always point scissors away from your body and keep hands away from the area in which you are cutting or punching holes.

1. Clean the clear 2 liter bottle.

2. Cut the bottle in half by carefully making a hole with the tip of your scissors where you will begin cutting and then inserting the tip of your scissors in the hole to cut the top off.

3. Poke holes in the bottom of the bottle to allow drainage using the tip of the scissors.

4. Fill the bottle bottom with potting soil.

5. Plant the Venus flytrap.

6. For the "lid," cut multiple 4-inch vertical slots around the bottom portion of the top half of the bottle to allow for airflow.

7. Stagger tucking every other slot in and out between the top and the bottom of the bottle.
    Discard the bottle cap. (The lid retains moisture and controls the temperature. The clear plastic allows for observation of root growth.)

Test. Observe your ecosystem every day and make notes in your STEM Research Notebook about it.

Decide. After you've observed your ecosystem, is there anything that could be improved upon? What improvements can you think of?

Share. Point out the interesting features of your ecosystem to your classmates. If you see the Venus flytrap doing something interesting, be sure to share that! Explain to your classmates how the design of your ecosystem helps your plant to thrive.

Team 4: Worker Worms
Page 1

Name:_____

Your team will create a worm farm!

You will create a home for your worms and make sure that their basic needs are met. Use the steps of the EDP to create your worm farm.

Define: What is the problem? _____

Learn: Do some research about your worms (ask your teachers for the name of your worm species):

- What do your worms need to eat? _____
- How will you feed them? _____
- Do they need water? How much? _____

Plan:

- Do you have all the supplies you need to build the farm? _____
- Who will take care of providing the food and water to the worms? You might want to create a schedule for team members to do these jobs.

    _____
    _____

Look at the building procedure and make a sketch of what your worm farm will look like on the back of this page.

Team 4: Worker Worms

Page 2

Name:_____

Try. Use this procedure to build your farm (don't forget to add the food you decided the ants need):

SAFETY NOTE: Always point scissors away from your body and keep hands away from the area in which you are cutting or punching holes.

1.   Clean the clear 2 liter bottle.

2.   Cut the top of the bottle off by carefully making a hole with the tip of your scissors where you will begin cutting and then inserting the tip of your scissors in the hole to cut the top off.

3.   Poke holes in the bottom of the bottle using the tip of your scissors to allow drainage.

4.   Add rocks to the bottom of the bottle.

5.   Alternate layers of sand and then potting soil until the layers reach close to the top, adding worms and banana peels within the layers.

6.   Put the bottle top back on (without the cap) to enable air flow. (The lid retains moisture and controls the temperature. The clear plastic allows for observation.)

7.   Keep in a cool dark place.

Test. Observe your worm farm every day and make notes in your STEM Research Notebook about it.

Decide. After you've observed your worm farm, is there anything that could be improved upon? Is it easy to feed your worms? If not, could you come up with a better system? What other improvements can you think of?

Share. Point out the interesting features of your worm farm to your classmates. If you see the worms doing something interesting, be sure to share that! Explain to your classmates how the design of your farm helps your worms to thrive.

Build Your Own Story Graphic Organizer

Name:_____

Solution

Setting

Characters

Problem

Lesson Plan 2:
Composting Systems

In this lesson, students will discover that there are a variety of systems for composting and will explore various benefits of composting. Students will observe how surface area is related to rates of decay for organic material and will explore the water content in organic materials. Student teams will research types of compost systems as a first step toward building a compost system prototype. Students will investigate byproducts of improperly aerated compost through an inquiry activity that demonstrates the production of methane from food waste. An optional field trip to a local composting center and/or recycling center will provide students with an opportunity to experience recycling and composting first-hand.

ESSENTIAL QUESTIONS

- What can compost be used for?

- What are the benefits of composting?

- How does surface area exposed to the air relate to rate of decay of organic material?

- What are commonly used types of compost systems?

- What materials are required to make a compost system?

- What conditions and care are necessary for compost systems?

- What impact do compost systems have on the environment, culture, and society?

- What are the byproducts of composting systems?

ESTABLISHED GOALS AND OBJECTIVES

At the conclusion of this lesson, students will be able to do the following:

- Describe microbes as a cause of decomposition and use this understanding to explain their observations of decomposition

- Predict, observe, and explain the relationship between the size of organic material and the rate of decomposition

- Identify multiple types of compost systems (wire-mesh holding unit, turning unit, heap, and worm compost)

- Identify and describe the components of a composting system

- Describe how elements of an ecosystem interact in a composting system

- Describe how composting systems are constructed

- Identify several uses of compost and use this knowledge to discuss the benefits of composting

- Describe the role of aeration in composting and identify the effects of lack of aeration in compost

- Apply their understanding of the role of oxygen in compost systems to create a compost plan that incorporates aeration

- Identify ideal conditions for composting in terms of aeration and size of food waste and apply this understanding to compost system plans

- Evaluate the impact compost systems have on the environment, culture, and society

- Apply their understanding of the engineering design process (EDP) to solving a problem

- Pose researchable questions and collect data about those questions

TIME REQUIRED

- 7 days (approximately 45 minutes each day; see Tables 3.7–3.8, p. 38)

MATERIALS

Required Materials for Lesson 2

- STEM Research Notebooks

- Computer with Internet access for viewing videos

- Computers with Internet access and presentation software for each team of 3–4 students

- Books

  o *Compost It* by David Barker
  o *Compost Center Operator* by Mirella S. Miller
  o *Fractions, Decimals, and Percents* by David A. Adler
  o *Who Was Franklin Roosevelt?* by Margaret Frith

- Chart paper

- Markers

Additional Materials for Room to Rot Activity (1 per class)

- 4 apples

- 1 knife

- 1 plastic bin about 15 inches deep

- Garden soil or potting soil (enough to fill the bin to at least 11 inches deep)

- Camera or other device for taking pictures

Additional Materials for Gas It Up Activity (1 per team of 3–4 students unless otherwise noted)

- Protective gloves (non-latex) (1 pair per student)

- 3 small-necked glass bottles (large enough to accommodate about 1 cup of material – glass beverage bottles, for example)

- 3 large balloons (about 12")

- Funnel

- 3 cups of soil

- Gallon-size Ziploc bag

- Duct tape

- Permanent marker

- Flexible tape measure

Additional Materials for Water Weight Demonstration (1 per class)

- Fruit scraps (for example, banana peel, apple slices, orange slices, cantaloupe)

- Baking pan

- Oven or food dehydrator

- Scale

SAFETY NOTES

1. Remind students that personal protective equipment (safety glasses or goggles, aprons, and gloves) must be worn during the setup, hands-on, and take-down segments of activities.

2. Caution students not to eat any materials used in activities.

3. Students should use caution when handling scissors as the sharp points and blades can cut or puncture skin.

4. Tell students to be careful when handling containers. Cans and cut plastic may have sharp edges, which can cut or puncture skin. Glass or plastic bottles can break and cut skin.

5. Immediately wipe up any spilled water or soil on the floor to avoid a slip-and-fall hazard.

6. Have students wash hands with soap and water after activities are completed.

CONTENT STANDARDS AND KEY VOCABULARY

Table 4.4 lists the content standards from the *NGSS*, *CCSS*, and the Framework for 21st Century Learning that this lesson addresses, and Table 4.5 presents the key vocabulary. Vocabulary terms are provided for both teacher and student use. Teachers may choose to introduce some or all of the terms to students.

Table 4.4. Content Standards Addressed in STEM Road Map Module Lesson 2

NEXT GENERATION SCIENCE STANDARDS

PERFORMANCE OBJECTIVES
- 5-ESS2–1. Develop a model using an example to describe ways the geosphere, biosphere, hydrosphere, and/or atmosphere interact.
- 5-ESS3–1. Obtain and combine information about ways individual communities use science ideas to protect the Earth's resources and environment.
- 5-ETS1–2. Generate and compare multiple possible solutions to a problem based on how well each is likely to meet the criteria and constraints of the problem.
- 5-LSW-1. Develop a model to describe the movement of matter among plants, animals, decomposers, and the environment.

DISCIPLINARY CORE IDEAS

ESS3.C: Human Impacts on Earth Systems
- Human activities in agriculture, industry, and everyday life have had major effects on the land, vegetation, streams, ocean, air, and even outer space. But individuals and communities are doing things to help protect Earth's resources and environment.

ETS1.B: Developing Possible Solutions
- Research on a problem should be carried out before beginning to design a solution. Testing a solution involves investigating how well it performs under a range of likely conditions.
- At whatever stage, communicating with peers about proposed solutions is an important part of the design process, and shared ideas can lead to improved designs.
- Tests are often designed to identify failure points or difficulties, which suggest the elements of the design that need to be improved.

Continued

Table 4.4. (*continued*)

CROSSCUTTING CONCEPTS

Systems and System Models
- A system is a group of related parts that make up a whole and can carry out functions its individual parts cannot.
- A system can be described in terms of its components and their interactions.

Cause and Effect
- Events have causes that generate observable patterns.
- Simple tests can be designed to gather evidence to support or refute student ideas about causes.

Influence of Science, Engineering, and Technology on Society and the Natural World
- People's needs and wants change over time, as do their demands for new and improved technologies.
- Engineers improve existing technologies or develop new ones to increase their benefits, decrease known risks, and meet societal demands.

SCIENCE AND ENGINEERING PRACTICES

Asking Questions and Defining Problems
- Ask questions about what would happen if a variable is changed.
- Identify scientific (testable) and non-scientific (non- testable) questions.
- Ask questions that can be investigated and predict reasonable outcomes based on patterns such as cause and effect relationships.
- Use prior knowledge to describe problems that can be solved.
- Define a simple design problem that can be solved through the development of an object, tool, process, or system and includes several criteria for success and constraints on materials, time, or cost.

Planning and Carrying Out Investigations
- Plan and conduct an investigation collaboratively to produce data to serve as the basis for evidence, using fair tests in which variables are controlled and the number of trials considered.
- Evaluate appropriate methods and/or tools for collecting data.
- Make observations and/or measurements to produce data to serve as the basis for evidence for an explanation of a phenomenon or test a design solution.
- Make predictions about what would happen if a variable changes.
- Test two different models of the same proposed object, tool, or process to determine which better meets criteria for success.

Obtaining, Evaluating, and Communicating Information
- Read and comprehend grade-appropriate complex texts and/or other reliable media to summarize and obtain scientific and technical ideas and describe how they are supported by evidence.
- Compare and/or combine across complex texts and/or other reliable media to support the engagement in other scientific and/or engineering practices.

- Combine information in written text with that contained in corresponding tables, diagrams, and/or charts to support the engagement in other scientific and/or engineering practices.
- Obtain and combine information from books and/or other reliable media to explain phenomena or solutions to a design problem.
- Communicate scientific and/or technical information orally and/or in written formats, including various forms of media as well as tables, diagrams, and charts.

COMMON CORE STATE STANDARDS FOR MATHEMATICS

MATHEMATICAL PRACTICES
- 5.MP1. Make sense of problems and persevere in solving them.
- 5.MP2. Reason abstractly and quantitatively.
- 5.MP3. Construct viable arguments and critique the reasoning of others.
- 5.MP4. Model with mathematics.
- 5.MP5. Use appropriate tools strategically.
- 5.MP6. Attend to precision.
- 5.MP7. Look for and make use of structure.
- 5.MP8. Look for and express regularity in repeated reasoning.

MATHEMATICAL CONTENT
- MD.C.5. Relate volume to the operations of multiplication and addition and solve real world and mathematical problems involving volume.

COMMON CORE STATE STANDARDS FOR ENGLISH LANGUAGE ARTS

READING STANDARDS
- RI.5.1. Quote accurately from a text when explaining what the text says explicitly and when drawing inferences from the text.
- RI.5.3. Explain the relationships or interactions between two or more individuals, events, ideas, or concepts in a historical, scientific, or technical text based on specific information in the text.
- RI.5.4. Determine the meaning of general academic and domain-specific words and phrases in a text relevant to a grade 5 topic or subject area.
- RI.5.7. Draw on information from multiple print or digital sources, demonstrating the ability to locate an answer to a question quickly or to solve a problem efficiently.
- RI.5.9. Integrate information from several texts on the same topic in order to write or speak about the subject knowledgeably.

WRITING STANDARDS
- W.5.1. Write opinion pieces on topics or texts, supporting a point of view with reasons and information.
- W.5.2. Write informative/explanatory texts to examine a topic and convey ideas and information clearly.
- W.5.4. Produce clear and coherent writing in which the development and organization are appropriate to task, purpose, and audience.

Continued

Table 4.4. (*continued*)

- W.5.6. With some guidance and support from adults, use technology, including the Internet, to produce and publish writing as well as to interact and collaborate with others; demonstrate sufficient command of keyboarding skills to type a minimum of two pages in a single sitting.
- W.5.7. Conduct short research projects that use several sources to build knowledge through investigation of different aspects of a topic.
- W.5.8. Recall relevant information from experiences or gather relevant information from print and digital sources; summarize or paraphrase information in notes and finished work, and provide a list of sources.

SPEAKING AND LISTENING STANDARDS
- SL.5.1. Engage effectively in a range of collaborative discussions (one-on-one, in groups, and teacher-led) with diverse partners on grade 5 topics and texts, building on others' ideas and expressing their own clearly.
- SL.5.4. Report on a topic or text or present an opinion, sequencing ideas logically and using appropriate facts and relevant, descriptive details to support main ideas or themes; speak clearly at an understandable pace.
- SL.5.5. Include multimedia components (for example, graphics, sound) and visual displays in presentations when appropriate to enhance the development of main ideas or themes.
- SL.5.6. Adapt speech to a variety of contexts and tasks, using formal English when appropriate to task and situation.

FRAMEWORK FOR 21ST CENTURY LEARNING
- Interdisciplinary themes (financial, economic, & business literacy; environmental literacy)
- Learning and Innovation Skills
- Information, Media & Technology Skills
- Life and Career Skills

Table 4.5. Key Vocabulary in Lesson 2

Key Vocabulary	Definition
aerobic	describes organisms that requires oxygen to live
anaerobic	describes organisms that can live without oxygen
conservation	the management of natural resources in order to preserve them
decomposition	to decay
element	a pure substance that cannot be broken down into other substances
fertile soil	soil that contains the nutrients that plants need to grow
hypothesis	an idea or prediction that can be tested

Key Vocabulary	Definition
microbe	a living organism that is not visible to the naked eye
nitrogen	a colorless and odorless element that is an important plant nutrient
nutrient	substances that a living thing uses as food
oxygen	an element in the air that has no color, smell, or taste but is necessary for plants and animals to live
potassium	an element that is a soft metal that interacts with air and water and is an important plant nutrient
phosphorous	an element that is an important plant nutrient
prototype	a model that is used to create a final product
rate	how quickly something happens

TEACHER BACKGROUND INFORMATION
Composting

In this lesson, students will consider the benefits of composting. Besides reducing the amount of solid waste in landfills, composting offers significant benefits in terms of the fertile soil it produces and in reducing the need for chemical fertilizers.

Soil health is influenced by the population of bacteria and fungi that live in the soil. These decomposers digest dead organic materials (for example, leaves dropping from trees and plant and animal remains), releasing nutrients that plants can use. Humus that contains nutrients and minerals necessary for plants is formed as acids produced by decomposers dissolve the outer layer of rocks.

The fertile layer of soil formed in the nutrient cycle described above is known as topsoil and may be a few inches to several feet thick. Topsoil can be depleted by erosion and activities such as farming that remove organic materials from the soil. Composting is one way to return these organic materials to the soil to ensure its fertility. In addition, plant death due to improper nutrients in the soil can result in erosion and further loss of topsoil. Building the topsoil with compost prevents erosion by encouraging the growth of plants. Fertile topsoil can also reduce the need for chemical fertilizers. Plants weakened by lack of soil nutrients may be more susceptible to disease. Treating the plants with chemicals such as pesticides and herbicides may have the side effect of also killing decomposers in the soil, further reducing plants' access to crucial nutrients and increasing the need for further chemical interventions.

Students will explore ideal conditions for a compost system. In particular, they will consider the relationship between size of food waste and rate of decay, water content, and aeration in decomposition.

COMMON MISCONCEPTIONS

Students will have various types of prior knowledge about the concepts introduced in this lesson. Table 4.6 outlines some common misconceptions students may have concerning these concepts. Because of the breadth of students' experiences, it is not possible to anticipate every misconception that students may bring as they approach this lesson. Incorrect or inaccurate prior understanding of concepts can influence student learning in the future, however, so it is important to be alert to misconceptions such as those presented in the table.

Table 4.6. Common Misconceptions About the Concepts in Lesson 2

Topic	Student Misconception	Explanation
Compost	Compost smells bad.	Compost only has an odor when it is too wet or when there is too much nitrogen in the compost. Maintaining a 2:1 balance between carbon containing "brown" matter and nitrogen-rich "green" matter will prevent odor.
Microbes	Microbes are "bad" and will make people sick.	There are many different types of microbes and only a small proportion of known microbes cause disease. In fact, microbes are a critical part of the environment and are necessary for our bodies to do things like digest food and fight disease-causing microbes. Microbes are used in foods and medicines and break down dead organic material.

PREPARATION FOR LESSON 2

Review the Teacher Background Information provided, assemble materials for the lesson, duplicate student handouts, and preview videos included within the Learning Plan Components. Students will use food waste (fruit and vegetable scraps) in the Gas It Up activity in this lesson. You should plan to have about 1½ cups of scraps per each group of three students.

If you plan to build a working compost system for your school, you should continue working with school staff and administration to make plans for the compost system. In particular, you should begin to consider the availability of financial resources for creating the compost system. If donations will be needed, you should begin contacting local businesses (see Lesson 4 Teacher Background Information for supplies needed for each type of compost system). You may also wish to ask students' families for donations of funds and supplies.

Student teams will research various types of compost systems in this lesson. Have books about compost systems available in the classroom and be prepared to direct students to the following websites if they need assistance in locating information or, alternatively, you may choose to print information from these sites to have available for student research:

- US Environmental Protection Agency (EPA), "Types of Composting and Understanding the Process": *www.epa.gov/sustainable-management-food/types-composting-and-understanding-process#vermi*

- Ohio State University Extension, "Composting at Home": *https://ohioline.osu.edu/factsheet/hyg-1189-99*

- Target Organics – A Compost Program Resource Hub: *https://hub.compost ingcouncil.org*

- University of Florida Extension, "Compost": *https://sfyl.ifas.ufl.edu/sarasota/natural-resources/waste-reduction/composting/*

- University of Georgia Extension Center for Urban Agriculture, "Building a Compost Mound": *https://ugaurbanag.com/building-a-compost-mound/*

- Louisiana State University Ag Center, "Wooden Box Bin": *www.lsuagcenter.com/portals/communications/publications/publications_catalog/lawn%20and%20garden/backyard%20composting/wooden-box-bin*

- Louisiana State University Ag Center, "Backyard Composting: Wood and Wire Three-Bin Turning Unit": *www.lsuagcenter.com/~/media/system/5/5/6/5/55651408db 63fb9691f6ae985bd9d2a7/pub2610iwoodandwirethreebinhighres.pdf*

- University of Missouri Extension, "How to Build a Compost Bin": *https:// extension2.missouri.edu/G6957*

LEARNING PLAN COMPONENTS
Introductory Activity/Engagement

Connection to the Challenge: Begin each day of this lesson by reminding students of the module challenge. Hold a brief student discussion of how their learning in the previous days' lesson(s) contributed to their ability to plan and build a prototype of a composting system.

Remind students of the steps of the EDP and ask them to complete the first step (Define) by identifying the problem presented in the module challenge. This will be a statement something like "The problem we want to solve is how to design and build a prototype of a compost system to reduce the amount of school food waste that goes to the landfill and to produce usable compost." Students will address the Learn step of the EDP in the Composting Containers activity (see Activity/Exploration section).

Science Class: Have students make observations of the four ecosystems created in Lesson 1 in their STEM Research Notebooks. Ask students to share what they noticed about the ecosystems – i.e., did they observe any change since their last observation?

Post the following quote by Charles Darwin: "All the fertile areas of this planet have at least once passed through the bodies of earthworms." Ask students to share their ideas about what this quote means, launching a discussion about fertile soil. Lead students to understand that fertile soil is soil that is able to support plant growth because it contains the nutrients that plants need to grow (primarily nitrogen, phosphorous, and potassium). Ask students for their ideas about how decomposers might help make soil fertile (they break down dead plant and animal material into the nutrients that plants need to grow).

Ask students for their ideas about what kinds of decomposers there are. Tell students that earthworms are decomposers and that other organisms too small to see are also decomposers. Introduce the term microbe and tell students that bacteria and fungi are types of microbes that decompose plant and animal material by eating it and then excreting materials from which the plants and animals were composed.

As a class, read aloud the book *Compost It* by David Barker. Hold a class discussion about composting, asking students:

- What are the reasons that people compost?

- How is compost used?

- What are the benefits of composting?

- What components are necessary for a compost system? (decomposers, organic material, oxygen, water)

- What influence do decomposers have on composting?

- What do compost systems produce?

- Why do compost bins need to be turned or ventilated?

Prompt students to understand that compost bins provide nutrient-rich compost that can be added to soil to help provide the nutrients that plants need to grow. Introduce the concept to students that the bacteria in compost bins need air to survive and do their decomposing work. Worms also help air to enter the compost.

Activity/Exploration

Science Class and Mathematics Connection: In this lesson, students will explore the relationship between size of food waste and how quickly the food decays (the Room to Rot activity). They will also explore the results of improper aeration in the Gas It Up activity, and will explore the volume of water in food waste in the Water Weight demonstration. There is an option for a field trip to a recycling center or composting center. Students will begin their research for the module challenge in this lesson as student teams investigate various types of composting systems in the Composting Containers activity.

Room to Rot

Students will use a predict, observe, explain cycle to explore the relationship between the size of organic material and the rate of decomposition. Students will create STEM Research Notebook entries for each phase of the process.

To introduce the activity, ask students if they have observed food decomposing. Ask students:

- What happens to food when it sits out in the air?

- What do you see?

- What do you smell?

- What causes this?

Show students a whole apple and tell them that they will predict how quickly apple pieces of different sizes will decompose. Puncture the skin of the second apple, cut the third apple into quarters, and cut the fourth apple into about 20 small pieces. Show students the apples and the container where they will be buried. Take a picture of each type of apple piece to be used for comparison as students observe the apples over time.

Distribute a copy of the Room to Rot student handout to each student. Have students record their predictions about which apple will decompose the fastest and which the slowest, how many days it will take for the apples to decompose completely (so that they are converted into fertile soil), and where the decomposition will begin on each apple. Bury the apples in the container of soil and mark where you buried each of the fruits by inserting a labeled craft stick over them. Dig up the apple pieces once every three to five days for the remainder of the module and take pictures, comparing the state of the apples and apple pieces to the previous pictures. Students should record their observations on their Room to Rot handouts and you should hold a class discussion asking students for their explanations for what they observe about the apples.

Gas It Up

In this activity, students will discover that gas is produced when compost is not aerated properly.

Have students brainstorm about what might happen if a compost pile is not turned (bacteria and other decomposers that need air to live will not be able to decompose the compost).

Tell students that bacteria that need air are called aerobic bacteria. These bacteria do much of the decomposition in compost. If there is not enough air available, they cannot do their work. There are, however, bacteria that do not need air to survive. These are called anaerobic bacteria.

Tell students that anaerobic bacteria live in the digestive systems of cows. Ask students what they know about what cows produce from their digestive systems besides poop (methane gas – cow farts).

Tell students that landfills also produce methane from the food waste that is buried deep within the landfill and does not get oxygen. This is similar to what would happen to food waste in a compost pile that is improperly aerated. Anaerobic composting is an option; however, it uses very different decomposing bacteria than does aerobic composting, and produces methane as a byproduct.

Tell students that they are going to produce methane from decomposing plants and will determine what, if any, effect, the surrounding environment has on methane production.

Point out to students that they cannot see microbes. Ask how they will be able to tell if the microbes are present (by the production of gas).

Ask students to make a hypothesis about what type of environmental conditions would cause decomposing plant material to produce methane the quickest? (for example, heat, cold, light, dark). Working in groups, students will have a chance to test their predictions over the next seven class periods. See the *Gas It Up* handouts at the end of this lesson plan for instructions.

Water Weight

Remind students of the nutrient cycle, and discuss as a class (using the diagram the class created in Lesson One) how the nutrient cycle might work in compost. Next, ask students to share their ideas about why they think water is important for composting systems. Lead students to understand that decomposers (bacteria, fungi, earthworms) need water to survive. If a compost pile is dry, therefore, the decomposers will die. Ask students what they think will happen if compost becomes very wet. Lead students to understand that if compost is too wet there will not be enough air for the aerobic bacteria to function.

Tell students that a moisture content of around 40–60% is considered ideal for most small composting systems. This feels like a wet (but not dripping) sponge to the touch. Show students a bag of fruit scraps (for example, a banana peel, apple slices, orange slices, cantaloupe pieces). Ask students whether there is water in these scraps and, if so, if this is enough water for a compost bin. Then ask students to share ideas about how they can measure the amount of water in food. Prompt students by asking them if water has weight and if they can think of a way to weigh the amount of water in the food.

Tell students that they are going to determine the moisture content of the fruit scraps by weighing the fruit with the water in it (the wet weight) and with the water removed from it (the dry weight). Ask students for ideas about how to remove water from the fruit scraps. Tell students that you will dehydrate the scraps by placing them in the oven for 24 hours (at about 135 degrees Fahrenheit). Alternatively, if you have a food dehydrator available you may choose to use that.

As a class, develop a procedure to determine the moisture content. The procedure may look something like this:

1. Find a container to heat the scraps in.

2. Measure the weight of the empty container.

3. Put the food scraps in the container.

4. Put the container with the food scraps in the oven.

5. Set the oven to 135 degrees Fahrenheit.

6. Leave the scraps in the oven for 24 hours.

7. Using hot pads, remove the food scraps from the oven.

8. Allow the container to cool.

9. Weigh the container.

10. Find the weight of the water removed (wet weight – dry weight).

11. Calculate the moisture content of the scraps using the following formula: moisture content = 100 × [(wet weight – dry weight) / wet weight].

Ask students to consider whether the amount of water in the fruit scraps would be enough to provide adequate moisture content for the compost. Compare the weight of the water in the scraps to five pounds of compost and have students calculate whether this weight is 40–60% of the weight of the compost.

Field Trip (Optional)

Arrange to take a field trip to a local composting and/or recycling center. Before the trip, have students brainstorm to create a list of questions to ask the center representatives. Prompt students to include questions about the type of composting systems the center uses in preparation for their investigation into types of compost systems in the next activity.

Composting Containers

Tell students that as part of their challenge for this module they will work in teams to create a prototype of a composting system. Remind students of the steps of the EDP. Review students' definition of the problem outlined in the module challenge (see Connection to the Challenge for this lesson, pp. 85–86). Tell students that the next thing they need to do is learn about various composting systems. Divide the class into teams of three to four students and have each team research one type of composting system using the graphic organizers attached at the end of this lesson plan. Note that there are four basic types of systems (holding unit, heap, turning unit, and worm composting bin) so it may be necessary for more than one team to research each system.

Student teams should collect information such as the following and record their findings in the graphic organizers:

- How does the compost system work?

- How is it set up?

- What materials do you need to make this type of system?

- How large does it need to be per pound of compost (for example, a worm bin requires one square foot per pound of food)?

- What kind of maintenance does it need (turning, etc.)?

- How expensive is it to buy or build?

Tell students to be sure to cite their sources (for example, websites, books, or articles). Each student will be responsible for creating a paper (about two pages) containing a written description of the composting system using the findings they record in their graphic organizers (see ELA Connection).

ELA Connection: Tell students that they each will write an essay to describe their team's assigned composting system to someone who is unfamiliar with this type of system. Students will use their findings from the Composting Containers activity. Tell students that this type of writing is called informative writing and its purpose is to give information to a reader.

Review the parts of an essay with students (thesis statement, introduction, middle, and conclusion). Ask students for their ideas about the types of information that should be included in the essay, creating a class list of student ideas. At a minimum, students should include the following:

- A description of the system

- A description of how the system works to create compost

- What kind of materials are used to build this kind of system

- What kind of maintenance the system requires

- Why someone might want to use this composting system

You may wish to provide students with a graphic organizer such as the Essay Graphic Organizer for a five-paragraph essay attached at the end of this lesson plan.

Social Studies Connection: Present students with this quote from Franklin Delano Roosevelt: "The nation that destroys its soil destroys itself." Hold a class discussion on what this quote means, relating soil quality to the importance of agriculture to society. You may wish to share the original context of this quote with students; Roosevelt's letter to state governors about the need for a soil conservation program can be found at *www.riceswcd.org/roosevelt-urges-states-to-create-conservation-districts/*.

Explanation

Science Class: After teams have finished their Composting Containers research, each team should create a sketch of the system labeling its parts and present this to the class, along with a brief presentation using a visual display with multimedia components (for example, a narrated PowerPoint presentation) providing the information they gained from their research. These presentations should include the list of sources students used in their research.

Mathematics Connection: Review percentages with the class by reading aloud as a class the book *Fractions, Decimals, and Percents* by David A. Adler. After reading the book, have students work in teams of two to four to create questions about characteristics of students in the class that can be expressed as percentages, encouraging students to ask questions for which all students will fall into a category (for example, what percentage of students are wearing shoes with laces? What percentage of students are wearing shoes without laces? What percentage of the class are boys? What percentage of the class are girls? What percentage of the class is wearing shirts with buttons? What percentage of the class is wearing shirts without buttons?). Check each team's question to ensure that the characteristic they chose can be easily counted and that their questions encompass all students in the class. Have students record their questions in their

STEM Research Notebooks with space after each question to record an answer. Next, give each team an opportunity to survey the class to find the answer to their questions by having students raise their hands in response to the questions, and have students record their findings in their notebooks.

After all teams have collected data, ask students for their ideas about what other information they need to know to calculate percentages (the total number of students in the class). Have teams work together to calculate percentages for the characteristic they chose and record their work and answers in their STEM Research Notebooks.

Next, ask students for their ideas about how they could express these findings using a graph. Students should conclude that a bar graph or a pie chart would be suitable for expressing these findings. Review bar graphs with students if necessary, and have students work in their teams to create bar graphs, labeling the bars with the characteristics they collected data about and the Y-axis with 0–100%. Each student should create a bar graph in his or her STEM Research Notebook.

ELA Connection: Pair each student with another student who researched and wrote their essay about a different type of composting system. Have students read each other's essays and provide feedback by responding to the following prompts on a blank sheet of paper.

- When I read the essay, I easily understood _____.

- I would have liked to read more about _____.

- From the description you provided, I think the composting system you described looks like (draw a picture using the information in the essay):

- Questions I have about the compost system after reading are _____.

Have students give their feedback to the authors of the essays.

Social Studies Connection: Hold a class discussion about Franklin Delano Roosevelt, asking students to share what they know about him and what questions they have about him, recording student responses on a class chart. As a class, read aloud the book *Who Was Franklin Roosevelt?* by Margaret Frith. After reading the book, hold a class discussion about what they learned about Franklin Roosevelt and why he was concerned about soil quality (to ensure that farmers could grow crops adequate to meet the nation's demands for food).

Elaboration/Application of Knowledge

Science Class: Have students look for evidence of recycling and composting around their homes and on their way to and from school. An optional activity is to have students conduct research to identify community programs that support composting and recycling in the community and that provide education to the community about composting. Based upon student findings you may wish to invite a guest speaker to talk to the class about various types of composting.

Have students revisit the "Need to Know" chart they created in their STEM Research Notebooks during Lesson 1. Ask students to add information to the chart. Hold a class discussion about what information students have gained and what they still need to know in order to address the module challenge.

Mathematics Connection: Show students a disposable water bottle and ask them to read the label to find out how the quantity of water is recorded on the bottle (liters or fluid ounces). Ask students if this measurement reflects weight. Remind students that in the Water Weight activity they calculated weights of water. Tell students that water and other liquids are commonly measured in volume. Ask students for ideas about how they can find the volume of the water if they know its weight. Show students the formula for density (density = mass/volume). Tell students that the density of water is the amount of water in a certain amount of space. We know that the density of water is 1 gram/mL – in other words, 1 gram of water occupies 1 milliliter of volume. Challenge students to use the density of water and the weight of the water they calculated in the Water Weight activity to find the volume of water they dehydrated from their food scraps.

ELA Connection: Have students revise and rewrite their composting system informative essay using the feedback they received from their partners.

Social Studies Connection: Introduce career connections. Ask students what careers they think are associated with composting and recycling, creating a class list of ideas. Read aloud the book *Compost Center Operator* by Mirella S. Miller and then hold a class discussion, asking students to share what they learned about the type of work compost center operators do and what kind of background and knowledge they need to have.

Evaluation/Assessment

Students may be assessed on the following performance tasks and other measures listed.

Performance Tasks

- Room to Rot handouts

- Gas It Up activity and handouts

- Composting Containers research

- Composting Containers presentation (see rubric in Appendix A)

- Composting Containers essays (see rubric in Appendix A)

Other Measures

- Teacher observations
- STEM Research Notebook entries
- Student participation in teams

INTERNET RESOURCES

Information about types of composting systems

- *www.epa.gov/sustainable-management-food/types-composting-and-understanding-process#vermi*
- https://hub.compostingcouncil.org
- *https://sfyl.ifas.ufl.edu/sarasota/natural-resources/waste-reduction/composting/*
- https://ugaurbanag.com/building-a-compost-mound/
- *www.lsuagcenter.com/portals/communications/publications/publications_catalog/lawn%20and%20garden/backyard%20composting/wooden-box-bin*
- *www.lsuagcenter.com/~/media/system/5/5/6/5/55651408db63fb9691f6ae985bd9d2a7/pub2610iwoodandwirethreebinhighres.pdf*
- *https://extension2.missouri.edu/G6957*
- *https://ohioline.osu.edu/factsheet/hyg-1189-99*

President Roosevelt's soil conservation letter

- *www.riceswcd.org/roosevelt-urges-states-to-create-conservation-districts/*

**Room to Rot
Student Handout (page 1/3)**

Name:_____

Make your predictions in the chart below. Circle the type of apple piece you think will decompose most quickly. Underline the type you think will decompose the slowest.

Type of Apple Piece	Predictions	
	Time to decompose completely?	Where on apple will we see the decomposition first?
Whole apple		
Apple with holes punched in skin		
Apple cut into quarters		
Apple cut into tiny pieces		

Whole Apple					
	Observation #				
	1	2	3	4	5
Draw a sketch of how the apple looks.					
Describe where the decomposition is happening on the apple.					

Room to Rot
Student Handout (page 2/3)

Name:_____

Apple with holes in skin					
	Observation #				
	1	2	3	4	5
Draw a sketch of how the apple looks.					
Describe where the decomposition is happening on the apple.					

Apple in quarters					
	Observation #				
	1	2	3	4	5
Draw a sketch of how the apple looks.					
Describe where the decomposition is happening on the apple.					

Room to Rot
Student Handout (page 3/3)

Name:_____

Smallest apple pieces					
	Observation #				
	1	2	3	4	5
Draw a sketch of how the apple looks.					
Describe where the decomposition is happening on the apple.					

Which type of apple pieces decomposed the most quickly? _____
_____
_____
_____

Were your predictions accurate? _____
_____
_____
_____

Gas It Up
Materials and Instructions

Materials:

Data sheet (1 per student)

3 small-necked glass bottles

3 large balloons

Disposable gloves

1 funnel

3 cups of soil

1½ cups of a mixture of fruit/vegetable scraps

Gallon-size Ziploc bag

Duct tape

Permanent marker

Flexible tape measure

Instructions:

1. Mix the soil and fruit/vegetable scraps thoroughly in a Ziploc bag.

2. Divide the mixture evenly between the three bottles, using the funnel to help you put the contents into the bottle.

3. Stretch a balloon over the opening of each bottle and secure it with duct tape.

4. Mark the initial level of the mixture on the bottle and mark the date.

5. Decide on three locations to place your bottle for observation (for instance, in sunlight, artificial light, near a heat source, in a refrigerator, in a dark place, etc.).

6. Label the bottom of each bottle with the name of your group and the location.

7. Place the bottles upright in each of the locations.

8. Record on your data sheet where you placed each bottle.

9. Make a predication about what you think will happen to the balloon circumferences and the heights of the mixtures in the bottles after 7 days. Record your predictions on your data sheet.

10. Observe the bottles every other day for 7 days. When you make your observation, mark the mixture level and the date. Measure the mixture levels and the balloon circumference and record the measurements on your data sheet.

11. After 7 days, answer the "Analyze" questions and graph your results.

12. After your measurements are complete, dispose of your mixtures outside and away from flames.

Gas It Up
Data Sheet, page 1

Name: _____

	Hypothesis What do you expect to observe about the material and the balloon after 7 days?	Observations			
		DAY 1	DAY 3	DAY 5	DAY 7
Bottle 1 Location:	Balloon Circumference: Mixture Height:	Balloon Circumference: Mixture Height:	Balloon Circumference: Mixture Height:	Balloon Circumference: Mixture Height:	Balloon Circumference: Mixture Height:
Bottle 2 Location:	Balloon Circumference: Mixture Height:	Balloon Circumference: Mixture Height:	Balloon Circumference: Mixture Height:	Balloon Circumference: Mixture Height:	Balloon Circumference: Mixture Height:
Bottle 3 Location:	Balloon Circumference: Mixture Height:	Balloon Circumference: Mixture Height:	Balloon Circumference: Mixture Height:	Balloon Circumference: Mixture Height:	Balloon Circumference: Mixture Height:

Gas It Up
Data Sheet, page 2

Analyze

1. In which locations did the balloons grow the biggest? Why?

2. In which locations did the balloons grow the least? Why?

3. Graph your results. Use the day of measurement on the X-axis and the balloon circumference on the Y-axis. Use different colors for each of the three different locations.

Holding Unit

Name:_____

Your team will be creating a prototype (a model) of a holding unit composting system for a school cafeteria to use. You will use the engineering design process (EDP) to do this.

Your first steps are to identify the problem and do some research.

What is the problem? What do you need to know to create a prototype? What information do you need? Record your answers to these questions in your STEM Research Notebook.

Imagine. It's time to do some research. Here are some questions to think about (record your answers in your STEM Research Notebook):

How does the compost system work?

Where is it typically used (homes, businesses, etc.)?

How is it set up?

What is it made of?

How large does it need to be per pound of compost?

What kind of maintenance does it need (turning, etc.)?

How expensive is it to buy or build?

Before you go any further you will share what you learned with the class. Create a drawing or diagram of the system to share with the class and be prepared to share with them what you learned from your research.

Turning Unit

Name:_____

Your team will be creating a prototype (a model) of a turning unit composting system for a school cafeteria to use. You will use the engineering design process (EDP) to do this.
Your first steps are to identify the problem and do some research.

What is the problem? What do you need to know to create a prototype? What information do you need? Record your answers to these questions in your STEM Research Notebook.

Imagine. It's time to do some research. Here are some questions to think about (record your answers in your STEM Research Notebook):

How does the compost system work?

Where is it typically used (homes, businesses, etc.)?

How is it set up?

What is it made of?

How large does it need to be per pound of compost?

What kind of maintenance does it need (turning, etc.)?

How expensive is it to buy or build?

Before you go any further you will share what you learned with the class. Create a drawing or diagram of the system to share with the class and be prepared to share with them what you learned from your research.

Heap

Name:_____

Your team will be creating a prototype (a model) of a heap composting system for a school cafeteria to use. You will use the engineering design process (EDP) to do this. Your first steps are to identify the problem and do some research.

What is the problem? What do you need to know to create a prototype? What information do you need? Record your answers to these questions in your STEM Research Notebook.

Imagine. It's time to do some research. Here are some questions to think about (record your answers in your STEM Research Notebook):

How does the compost system work?

Where is it typically used (homes, businesses, etc.)?

How is it set up?

What is it made of?

How large does it need to be per pound of compost?

What kind of maintenance does it need (turning, etc.)?

How expensive is it to buy or build?

Before you go any further you will share what you learned with the class. Create a drawing or diagram of the system to share with the class and be prepared to share with them what you learned from your research.

Worm Bin

Name:_____

Your team will be creating a prototype (a model) of a worm bin composting system for a school cafeteria to use. You will use the engineering design process (EDP) to do this.

Your first steps are to identify the problem and do some research.

What is the problem? What do you need to know to create a prototype? What information do you need? Record your answers to these questions in your STEM Research Notebook.

Imagine. It's time to do some research. Here are some questions to think about (record your answers in your STEM Research Notebook):

How does the compost system work?

Where is it typically used (homes, businesses, etc.)?

How is it set up?

What is it made of?

How large does it need to be per pound of compost?

What kind of maintenance does it need (turning, etc.)?

How expensive is it to buy or build?

Before you go any further you will share what you learned with the class. Create a drawing or diagram of the system to share with the class and be prepared to share with them what you learned from your research.

Essay Graphic Organizer

Name:_____

Introduction *(thesis statement and description of what you will do in the essay)*	
Paragraph 2 *(introduce the first topic and provide details)*	
Paragraph 3 *(introduce the second topic and provide details)*	
Paragraph 4 *(introduce the fourth topic and provide details)*	
Paragraph 5 *(conclusion and summary)*	

Lesson Plan 3:
Prototyping Compost Systems

In this lesson, students will design and build prototypes of the composting systems they investigated in Lesson 2. Students will use mathematical concepts to scale their prototype to an outdoor area that is accessible to the school cafeteria. Teams will create budgets for full-scale versions of the compost system they are prototyping. The class will also work to plan a publicity campaign to promote composting to students and staff at the school. In addition, students will apply their understanding of composting to create their own worm composting bins for personal use.

ESSENTIAL QUESTIONS

- How can we measure and plot out a space for a compost system?

- How can we use the EDP to build a compost system prototype?

- How can we communicate the importance of composting to our school community?

ESTABLISHED GOALS AND OBJECTIVES

At the conclusion of this lesson, students will be able to do the following:

- Create scaled drawings of a compost system

- Apply their understanding of how compost systems are designed and constructed to create a compost system prototype

- Use the EDP to create a compost system prototype

- Explain important features of their composting system

- Create a budget for building a full-scale composting system

- Identify the elements of publicity campaigns and apply these elements to create a campaign for composting at their school

- Apply their understanding of composting principles to create individual worm composters

TIME REQUIRED

5 days (approximately 30 minutes each day; see Table 3.9, p. 39)

MATERIALS

Required Materials for Lesson 3

- STEM Research Notebooks
- Computer with Internet access for viewing videos
- Books
  - o *Perimeter, Area, and Volume: A Monster Book of Dimensions* by David Adler
  - o *Rotten Pumpkin* by David Schwartz
- Chart paper
- Markers

Additional Materials for Measure It

- Retractable tape measures (1 per team)
- Graph paper (1–4 sheets per student, depending on scale used)
- Ruler (1 per student)

Additional Materials for Prototype It (1 per team of 3–4 students unless otherwise noted)

- Foam board for base of prototype – 15″ x 20″
- 8″ ×10″ pieces of cardstock or poster board – 6
- Craft sticks – 20
- Craft glue
- Masking tape
- Scissors – 2
- Drinking straws – 10
- Pipe cleaners – 10
- 22-gauge floral wire – 5 feet
- Large paper clips – 10
- Construction paper – 5 sheets
- Plastic knives – 2
- Toothpicks – 10
- Modeling clay – 8 ounces

- Cotton balls – 10

- Paint brushes – 2

- Craft paint – various colors available for students to choose from

Additional Materials for Wonderful Worms (per student)

- 2 – 32 oz. plastic containers, 1 with a lid

- Dark-colored opaque paint or spray paint for plastic (dark green or blue) – about 1 can per 10 students

- Paint brush (if non-spray paint is used)

- Disposable non-latex gloves

- Protective eyewear (safety glasses)

- Composting worms – 5

- Paper towels – 5 full size

- Small rocks or gravel – about ¼ cup per student

- Shredded newspaper (a plastic grocery bag about ½ full)

- Garden soil – about 2 cups

- Small pieces of fruit waste (banana peel, shredded carrot) – about 2½ tsp. per day for a week

SAFETY NOTES

1. Remind students that personal protective equipment (safety glasses or goggles, aprons, and gloves) must be worn during the setup, hands-on, and take-down segments of activities.

2. Caution students not to eat any materials used in activities.

3. Students should use caution when handling scissors as the sharp points and blades can cut or puncture skin.

4. If students will be using a drill or other hand tools in this lesson, be sure to provide protective work gloves, demonstrate how the tool is used, and supervise students closely.

5. Tell students to be careful when handling containers. Cans and cut plastic may have sharp edges, which can cut or puncture skin. Glass or plastic bottles can break and cut skin.

6. Instruct students to be aware of and avoid poisonous plants and insects, any refuse, sharps (broken glass), and other hazards when they are outdoors.

7. Immediately wipe up any spilled water or soil on the floor to avoid a slip-and-fall hazard.

8. Have students wash hands with soap and water after activities are completed.

CONTENT STANDARDS AND KEY VOCABULARY

Table 4.7 lists the content standards from the *NGSS*, *CCSS*, and the Framework for 21st Century Learning that this lesson addresses, and Table 4.8 presents the key vocabulary. Vocabulary terms are provided for both teacher and student use. Teachers may choose to introduce some or all of the terms to students.

Table 4.7. Content Standards Addressed in STEM Road Map Module Lesson 3

NEXT GENERATION SCIENCE STANDARDS

PERFORMANCE OBJECTIVES

- 5-ESS2–1. Develop a model using an example to describe ways the geosphere, biosphere, hydrosphere, and/or atmosphere interact.
- 5-ESS3–1. Obtain and combine information about ways individual communities use science ideas to protect the Earth's resources and environment.
- 5-LSW-1. Develop a model to describe the movement of matter among plants, animals, decomposers, and the environment.
- 5-ETS1–2. Generate and compare multiple possible solutions to a problem based on how well each is likely to meet the criteria and constraints of the problem.
- 5-ETS1–3. Plan and carry out fair tests in which variables are controlled and failure points are considered to identify aspects of a model or prototype that can be improved.

DISCIPLINARY CORE IDEAS

ESS3.C: Human Impacts on Earth Systems
- Human activities in agriculture, industry, and everyday life have had major effects on the land, vegetation, streams, ocean, air, and even outer space. But individuals and communities are doing things to help protect Earth's resources and environment.

ETS1.A: Defining and Delimiting Engineering Problems
- Possible solutions to a problem are limited by available materials and resources (constraints). The success of a designed solution is determined by considering the desired features of a solution (criteria). Different proposals for solutions can be compared on the basis of how well each one meets the specified criteria for success or how well each takes the constraints into account.

ETS1.B: Developing Possible Solutions
- Research on a problem should be carried out before beginning to design a solution. Testing a solution involves investigating how well it performs under a range of likely conditions.
- At whatever stage, communicating with peers about proposed solutions is an important part of the design process, and shared ideas can lead to improved designs.
- Tests are often designed to identify failure points or difficulties, which suggest the elements of the design that need to be improved.

ETS1.C: Optimizing the Design Solution
- Different solutions need to be tested in order to determine which of them best solves the problem, given the criteria and the constraints.

CROSSCUTTING CONCEPTS

Systems and System Models
- A system is a group of related parts that make up a whole and can carry out functions its individual parts cannot.
- A system can be described in terms of its components and their interactions.

Cause and Effect
- Events have causes that generate observable patterns.
- Simple tests can be designed to gather evidence to support or refute student ideas about causes.

Influence of Science, Engineering, and Technology on Society and the Natural World
- People's needs and wants change over time, as do their demands for new and improved technologies.
- Engineers improve existing technologies or develop new ones to increase their benefits, decrease known risks, and meet societal demands.

SCIENCE AND ENGINEERING PRACTICES

Asking Questions and Defining Problems
- Ask questions about what would happen if a variable is changed.
- Identify scientific (testable) and non-scientific (non-testable) questions.
- Ask questions that can be investigated and predict reasonable outcomes based on patterns such as cause and effect relationships.
- Use prior knowledge to describe problems that can be solved.
- Define a simple design problem that can be solved through the development of an object, tool, process, or system and includes several criteria for success and constraints on materials, time, or cost.

Planning and Carrying Out Investigations
- Plan and conduct an investigation collaboratively to produce data to serve as the basis for evidence, using fair tests in which variables are controlled and the number of trials considered.

Continued

Table 4.7. (*continued*)

- Evaluate appropriate methods and/or tools for collecting data.
- Make observations and/or measurements to produce data to serve as the basis for evidence for an explanation of a phenomenon or test a design solution.
- Make predictions about what would happen if a variable changes.
- Test two different models of the same proposed object, tool, or process to determine which better meets criteria for success.

Constructing Explanations and Designing Solutions
- Construct an explanation of observed relationships (for example, the distribution of plants in the back yard).
- Use evidence (for example, measurements, observations, patterns) to construct or support an explanation or design a solution to a problem.
- Identify the evidence that supports particular points in an explanation.
- Apply scientific ideas to solve design problems.
- Generate and compare multiple solutions to a problem based on how well they meet the criteria and constraints of the design solution.

Obtaining, Evaluating, and Communicating Information
- Read and comprehend grade-appropriate complex texts and/or other reliable media to summarize and obtain scientific and technical ideas and describe how they are supported by evidence.
- Compare and/or combine across complex texts and/or other reliable media to support the engagement in other scientific and/or engineering practices.
- Combine information in written text with that contained in corresponding tables, diagrams, and/or charts to support the engagement in other scientific and/or engineering practices.
- Obtain and combine information from books and/or other reliable media to explain phenomena or solutions to a design problem.
- Communicate scientific and/or technical information orally and/or in written formats, including various forms of media as well as tables, diagrams, and charts.

COMMON CORE STATE STANDARDS FOR MATHEMATICS

MATHEMATICAL PRACTICES
- 5.MP1. Make sense of problems and persevere in solving them.
- 5.MP2. Reason abstractly and quantitatively.
- 5.MP3. Construct viable arguments and critique the reasoning of others.
- 5.MP4. Model with mathematics.
- 5.MP5. Use appropriate tools strategically.
- 5.MP6. Attend to precision.
- 5.MP7. Look for and make use of structure.
- 5.MP8. Look for and express regularity in repeated reasoning.

MATHEMATICAL CONTENT

- MD.A.1. Convert among different-sized standard measurement units within a given measurement system (for example, convert 5 cm to 0.05 m), and use these conversions in solving multi-step, real world problems.
- MD.C.5. Relate volume to the operations of multiplication and addition and solve real world and mathematical problems involving volume.

COMMON CORE STATE STANDARDS FOR ENGLISH LANGUAGE ARTS

READING STANDARDS

- RI.5.1. Quote accurately from a text when explaining what the text says explicitly and when drawing inferences from the text.
- RI.5.3. Explain the relationships or interactions between two or more individuals, events, ideas, or concepts in a historical, scientific, or technical text based on specific information in the text.
- RI.5.4. Determine the meaning of general academic and domain-specific words and phrases in a text relevant to a grade 5 topic or subject area.
- RI.5.7. Draw on information from multiple print or digital sources, demonstrating the ability to locate an answer to a question quickly or to solve a problem efficiently.
- RI.5.9. Integrate information from several texts on the same topic in order to write or speak about the subject knowledgeably.

WRITING STANDARDS

- W.5.1. Write opinion pieces on topics or texts, supporting a point of view with reasons and information.
- W.5.2. Write informative/explanatory texts to examine a topic and convey ideas and information clearly.
- W.5.4. Produce clear and coherent writing in which the development and organization are appropriate to task, purpose, and audience.
- W.5.6. With some guidance and support from adults, use technology, including the Internet, to produce and publish writing as well as to interact and collaborate with others; demonstrate sufficient command of keyboarding skills to type a minimum of two pages in a single sitting.
- W.5.7. Conduct short research projects that use several sources to build knowledge through investigation of different aspects of a topic.
- W.5.8. Recall relevant information from experiences or gather relevant information from print and digital sources; summarize or paraphrase information in notes and finished work, and provide a list of sources.

SPEAKING AND LISTENING STANDARDS

- SL.5.1. Engage effectively in a range of collaborative discussions (one-on-one, in groups, and teacher-led) with diverse partners on grade 5 topics and texts, building on others' ideas and expressing their own clearly.

Continued

Table 4.7. *(continued)*

- SL.5.4. Report on a topic or text or present an opinion, sequencing ideas logically and using appropriate facts and relevant, descriptive details to support main ideas or themes; speak clearly at an understandable pace.
- SL.5.5. Include multimedia components (for example, graphics, sound) and visual displays in presentations when appropriate to enhance the development of main ideas or themes.
- SL.5.6. Adapt speech to a variety of contexts and tasks, using formal English when appropriate to task and situation.

FRAMEWORK FOR 21ST CENTURY LEARNING
Interdisciplinary themes (financial, economic, & business literacy; environmental literacy); Learning and Innovation Skills; Information, Media & Technology Skills; Life and Career Skills

Table 4.8. Key Vocabulary for Lesson 3

Key Vocabulary	Definition
audience	the people who will receive a written or spoken message
campaign	actions that are planned and performed with the objective of achieving a goal
container garden	a garden where plants grow in pots or other containers rather than in the ground
mood	the feeling that a reader has when reading a piece of writing that is created by the kind of language and writing the author uses
publicity	providing information to the public to raise awareness of products, services, or issues
rooftop garden	a garden that is planted on the roof of a building
scale	the amount by which a drawing or model is made smaller or larger as compared to the original
urban garden	growing plants in a city with limited space for farming or gardening

TEACHER BACKGROUND INFORMATION

Students will continue to use the EDP in this lesson as they create prototypes of composting systems based upon their findings in the *Learn* step of the EDP in the last lesson.

Students will create individual, portable compost systems during this lesson. These will be mini worm composting bins and can be maintained for about a week. After one week, students should either move the worms into a larger worm composting bin or add them and the compost to a garden.

COMMON MISCONCEPTIONS

Students will have various types of prior knowledge about the concepts introduced in this lesson. Table 4.9 outlines some common misconceptions students may have concerning these concepts. Because of the breadth of students' experiences, it is not possible to anticipate every misconception that students may bring as they approach this lesson. Incorrect or inaccurate prior understanding of concepts can influence student learning in the future, however, so it is important to be alert to misconceptions such as those presented in the table.

Table 4.9. Common Misconceptions About the Concepts in Lesson 3

Topic	Student Misconception	Explanation
Worm composting	All food waste can be composted by worms.	Meats, fats, dairy items, and junk food should not be composted; also, citrus fruit waste should not be added to worm compost bins because some varieties of worms will not eat them.
Prototypes	Prototypes must be fully functioning small versions of the thing they represent.	Prototypes should show the important components of the item they represent; however, they do not need to be fully functional.

PREPARATION FOR LESSON 3

Review the Teacher Background Information provided, assemble the materials for the lesson, make copies of the student handouts, and preview the videos recommended in the Learning Plan Components section below. Identify an area for the compost system (or if you are not building a full-sized system as part of this module, identify an area that could be used for a full-sized compost system) so that students can take measurements and scale their prototypes appropriately. Since students will need to work outdoors to measure the area designated for the school compost system, you should check the weather report and plan accordingly. Also prepare a time for students to visit the school cafeteria to gain an understanding of the flow of food waste and to identify outdoor exits.

Decide ahead of time what units students will use to take measurements of the compost system area (feet or inches are the units used on most retractable tape measures).

The concept of scale may be difficult for some students to grasp. You may wish to have a road map on hand and prepare to use map scale as an example.

Assemble the prototype building materials in advance and display a set of materials in such a way that students can view them as they create a materials list for building their prototypes.

The mini worm composting bins students will create in this lesson require small bits of fruit or vegetable waste (each worm requires about half its weight in food daily so each bin will require approximately 2 teaspoons of food scraps each day). Note that citrus peels are toxic to worms so you should ensure that no citrus scraps are included in the waste to be added to the worm composting bins. Tiny bits of banana peel work well. The inner plastic containers used in the worm composting bins will need to have small holes in the bottom for drainage and the lids will have to have small holes for air circulation. You may wish to create these holes in advance by drilling six to seven holes with a small drill bit. In addition, the outer container and lid should be painted a dark color to shield the worms from light. You may wish to do this in advance. If you have students spray paint their own containers, make sure to have available an outdoor space that is well ventilated and cover the ground beneath and surrounding the containers with newspaper. It may require several coats of paint to achieve an opaque covering. You will also need to have a large bowl of water or other water source in your classroom for students to wet their shredded newspaper.

Students will create a publicity campaign for composting to share with the school community. Prepare for this by collecting brochures or other publicity items from local recycling programs or other local campaigns related to environmental health to have on hand as examples.

Students will create budgets for a full-size version of their team's composting system during this lesson. Be prepared with materials price lists from area hardware stores or be prepared to have students research materials prices on the Internet. Although students will not build full-size versions of each composting system prototype, in the case that the class builds a full-scale compost system they will be able to apply their understanding of budgets and materials costs to this system. An option for this activity is to have students use spreadsheet software to create their budgets. If you choose to have students use the software, ensure that each student team has access to a computer with the appropriate software loaded on it.

LEARNING PLAN COMPONENTS
Introductory Activity/Engagement

Connection to the Challenge: Begin each day of this lesson by reminding students of the module challenge. Hold a brief student discussion of how their learning in the previous days' lesson(s) contributed to their ability to plan and build a prototype of a composting system.

Science Class: Review the steps of the EDP and remind students that they have completed the first steps (Define and Learn) by identifying the problem presented in the module challenge and conducting background research on composting systems. In this lesson, students will address the *Plan* and *Try* steps by creating a prototype composting system.

Continue to have students make periodic observations of the four ecosystems they created in Lesson 1 and record their observations in their STEM Research Notebooks. Ask students to share what they noticed about the ecosystems – i.e., did they observe any change since their last observation or since the first day?

Also, as a class continue to make observations every three to five days about how the apple pieces are decomposing in the Room to Rot activity from Lesson 2. Have students record their observations on the Room to Rot student handout.

As a class, read the book *Rotten Pumpkin* by David Schwartz. You may wish to have students act as the "voices" of the various animals and decomposers throughout the story. After the reading, ask students what surprised them about the story (for example, fly vomit dissolves pumpkin matter so the flies can eat it, how penicillin works).

Ask students whether or not the pumpkin is an ecosystem. Have students name the biotic and abiotic factors they noticed in the book and create a class list of these factors. Have students create a STEM Research Notebook entry in which they compare and contrast the rotting pumpkin ecosystem with a compost heap ecosystem. You may wish to have students use a Venn diagram.

Mathematics Connections: Ask students how much they think it will cost to build a full-scale version of the compost systems their teams are prototyping. Provide an example of a unit that can hold about ten pounds of food waste per day (this is roughly equivalent to one 4' ×4' × 4' compost bin). Record student cost estimates by the type of container each team is prototyping.

Point out to students that these costs are just guesses and that it is important to understand the costs of a building project in advance. Ask students for ideas about how they might find out how much the systems will actually cost. Introduce the idea of a budget as an informed estimate of expenses and income for a period of time or for a specific project. Tell students that they will create budgets for full-sized compost systems during this lesson.

ELA Connection: After reading the book *Rotten Pumpkin* by David Schwartz, compare and contrast the voices of several characters. Ask students: How does the author use language to differentiate between characters? Introduce the concepts of mood in literature (the atmosphere created by the author's words). Have students provide one-word descriptions for the mood created for several characters (for example, excited, sad, worried, informative).

Introduce the concept that different types of language are used for different purposes in writing. Have students brainstorm ideas about the various purposes of writing (for example, to entertain, to convey information, to persuade people to do or believe something). Ask students if they have seen any information published on recycling and what kind of language that information used (informative, persuasive). Show students the publicity materials from a local recycling campaign or materials from another organization related to environmental health you assembled. Read aloud portions of text from these materials, asking students to identify how the author used language to inform and persuade readers. Tell students that in this lesson they will create materials for the school to inform students and teachers about composting and persuade them to consider composting food waste at school and in their own homes.

Review the sample printed publicity materials and have students identify the components of the campaign. Make sure that students identify logos, slogans, informational text, persuasive text, graphics and pictures, links to outside resources, and other elements of the printed materials.

Social Studies Connection: Ask students to share their ideas about ways that composting is good for the community. Extend the discussion to include student ideas about how compost created from a school composting system could be used for the school community or the community at large (for example, if there is a school garden, compost can be added to fertilize soil).

Activity/Exploration

Science Class: Students will continue to move through the steps of the EDP to build their compost system prototypes in this lesson. Begin by watching the video "How to Use Compost" at *www.youtube.com/watch?v=NpdoftbXPVk*. Ask students to watch for information that might be useful to them as they build their compost system prototypes.

Next, ask students for their ideas about what they need to know about the compost system's location. Tell students that they will consider the space available and collect information to create scaled prototype drawings in the Measure It activity and then will build their prototypes in the Prototype It activity.

Measure It

Ask students what some limitations to composting are (for example, ask "why doesn't everyone compost?"). Create a list of these limitations. Be sure that students include space limitations on the list.

Remind students that in previous lessons they completed the *Define* phase of the EDP and collected information for the *Learn* phase. Ask students to name the next steps of the EDP (*Plan* and *Try*). Tell students that in this phase they will create a design and plan to build their prototypes, but that first they need to understand how much space they have to work with in the real world. Introduce the idea that when engineers create their drawings and prototypes or models they are made to scale. Introduce to students that scale is a way to represent large areas in a small space. The simplest way to represent scale for this activity will be to establish a standard scale such as 1 inch = 1 foot. Tell students that engineers use scale to draw their designs before they build them.

Ask students what measurements are important when deciding on how much space something like a composting system will occupy. Introduce the concepts of area and perimeter. Read the book *Perimeter, Area, and Volume: A Monster Book of Dimensions* by David Adler aloud as a class. Ask students what measurements they think are important for their composting systems. While volume is an important consideration for such systems, scaled volume calculations are beyond the scope of this module, so students will focus on the perimeter of the available area.

Take a trip to the school cafeteria to determine what the flow of food waste is there, and where the kitchen's closest outside exits are. Visit the area you identified in which a school composting system could be built.

Have each student create a scaled diagram on graph paper of the space available for the composting system. Have students measure the length and width of the available space and draw the area to scale on graph paper, designating a scale such as 5 graph paper blocks = 1 foot or 1 inch = 1 foot. Depending on the scale used, students may need to use multiple pieces of graph paper and tape them together. Instruct students to include features such as building walls, doors, sidewalks, and trees on their diagrams.

Prototype It

Student teams will each create a prototype of their assigned composting system in this activity. Students should understand that a prototype is a preliminary model on which a final product is based. They should understand that a prototype is a small-scale model of an object used to develop full-scale versions. Prototypes need not be working models, but should be representative of what a final product will look like and should contain the important functional features.

Teams should use the diagrams of the outdoor space they created in the Measure It activity and create a scaled model of their team's composting system. Students will continue to use the EDP as they proceed through the activity. Remind students that they completed the first steps of the EDP in previous lessons when they identified the problem and researched their composting system. Tell students that they are now completing the *Plan* and *Try* phases of the EDP and will also complete the Test and Decide steps as they finish constructing their prototypes. Students should use the Prototype It graphic organizer attached at the end of this lesson plan to organize their work.

Mathematics Connection: Review the concepts of area and perimeter introduced in the Measure It activity and the book *Perimeter, Area, and Volume: A Monster Book of Dimensions*. Provide student teams with tape measures and challenge them to calculate areas for defined areas (their desk, the classroom, the door, etc.).

Continue the discussion of budgeting from the Introductory Activity/Engagement. Ask students to share their ideas about how to make a budget. Lead students to an understanding that creating their budget will be a process that will include the following steps:

1. Create a materials list using the research they conducted in Lesson Two.

2. Research costs of materials and find unit costs.

3. Calculate total costs for each material.

4. Calculate total costs for all materials.

5. Create a list of income sources.

6. Total the amount of income.

7. If income is less than expenses, decide how to balance the budget (either reduce expenses or raise additional money).

Have student teams work through the budget process and create a budget for a full-size version of their composting system using a template such as the Composting System Budget student handout attached at the end of the lesson plan or spreadsheet software.

ELA Connection: Student teams will create printed materials for a composting campaign for their school. Ask students for their ideas about what message their campaign should convey (for example, why composting is a good idea, how to compost). Ask students to share ideas about what elements should be included in their materials (for example, logo, slogan, pictures, text). An option is to hold a class contest for a slogan and a logo for the campaign that all teams will use in their materials. Each team should decide whether to create pamphlets for reproduction or posters or flyers.

Have student teams brainstorm ideas about what type of information should be included in the printed materials. After teams have had 5 minutes to brainstorm, have each team share their ideas with the class, creating a class list of information students identify. Hold a class discussion about what the most important pieces of information to include are.

Show students some of the brochures and materials you assembled and ask them what they notice about how it looks (for example, how the text is arranged, how pictures are used, how much information is presented on each page). Create a class list of characteristics students identify. Introduce the idea of audience and ask students who their audience will be for their materials. Emphasize to students that it is important to use language that their audience can easily understand and that the information be easy to read and visually appealing.

Social Studies Connection: Hold a class discussion about the challenges of composting, asking students to name challenges, creating a class list. Explain to students that activities such as composting or gardening can be particularly difficult in urban areas where space is limited. Introduce the idea of urban gardening. Show students a video about urban gardening such as "Urban Farm" at *www.youtube.com/watch?v=qJAnBGHhjAc*.

Explanation

Science Class: After students have completed their prototypes, teams should present them to the class, highlighting the important features of the system. Students should include information about the care and maintenance of this type of composting system.

Mathematics Connection: Have each team share the budget it created with the class. Have teams explain how they arrived at their cost estimates and income estimates and explain whether, based on their budget, they think they will have enough resources to build their compost system.

ELA Connection: Have each student team create its composting publicity materials, and then have each team share their product with the class.

Social Studies Connection: Ask students to name some particular challenges for composting and gardening in urban areas and to brainstorm some solutions for these challenges.

Introduce students to the concepts of rooftop and container gardening as ways to grow plants in small spaces. Explain to students that composting can also be done on a small scale in inside spaces using closed containers. Also, explain to students that some municipalities offer community food-waste collection for composting on a regular basis.

Elaboration/Application of Knowledge

Science Class: Revisit the "Need to Know" chart students created in Lesson 1. Have students add information from this lesson to the chart. Ask students if there is any information missing from the chart. If you will be building a full-scale school composting system, this will be done in the next lesson, so it is important that students have all the information they need to build a full-scale composting system at this point.

Students will create their own worm composting bins in the Wonderful Worms activity and make observations for about a week. Show a time-lapse video of worms making compost as an introduction to the activity (for example, "Worms at Work: 20 Days Timelapse of Vermiposting" at *www.youtube.com/watch?v=n9Mnf9ysNSs*). Ask students what they observed during the video; what changes did they see over the 20 days?

Next, show students a video about creating a vermiposting compost system such as the following video from PBS Learning Media "Worm Farm" at *https://gpb.pbslearn ingmedia.org/resource/3daedfdc-edec-4c2e-b301-850cb5a8653e/3daedfdc-edec-4c2e-b301-850cb5a8653e/*. Tell students that they are going to create their own worm composting farms (mini worm composting bins) in this lesson. Ask students to share what important information they learned about maintaining a worm farm.

Wonderful Worms

Show the students two of the 32-ounce containers. Have students brainstorm ideas about how they could build contained, neat worm composting bins that can be used indoors.

Next, give each student two containers and one lid. Students will need an outer container (this is what will be painted) and an inner container that has holes in the bottom and in the lid. Give students one or two small rocks or a small amount of gravel (enough to cover the bottom of the outer container). Ask students how they think that they can use these to create a composting bin. If you did not pre-drill the holes in the lids, you should have students do this now.

If you did not paint the outer containers and lids in advance, have students paint them (note, if students will spray paint their containers, ensure that students' skin and eyes are protected). Keep in mind that several coats may be necessary to create an opaque surface. It is not necessary to wait for the paint to dry completely between coats.

While the paint dries, assist students in creating small holes in the bottom of the inner container. Be sure that the holes are small enough that the worms can't escape. Ensure that students' eyes and hands are protected.

After the outer container paint is dry, have students place their rocks or gravel in the bottom. Next, have students line the bottom of their inner container with a paper towel and place the inner container inside the outer container. Ask students why they think they are placing the paper towel there (to prevent worms and worm poop from escaping the container).

Give each student shredded newspaper (enough to fill about half a plastic grocery bag). Have students quickly dip the newspaper into water and remove it, squeezing out the excess water. The newspaper will be part of the worm's bedding, so they need to be able to move through it; have students fluff the newspaper before adding it to the inner container. The newspaper should fill the container about ½ to ¾ full.

Next, give each student very small bits of banana peel or other fruit scraps. Have students bury the food in various spots throughout the shredded newspaper. Have each student select five worms and add them to the inner container. Ask students to observe what the worms do when they are in the container (they will probably burrow into the newspaper to escape the light). Next, put a layer of garden soil on top and place the lid on the container.

Discuss with students how the requirements for composting bins (aeration, water, organic material) are being met in this composting bin. Students should make daily observations of their worm compost bins for one week and record these observations in their STEM Research Notebooks.

Make sure that students understand how to care for and feed their worms. The worms will eat half of their weight in fruit or vegetable scraps daily. This requires that a small amount of food be added to the top every two to three days (check to be sure that the food is gone before adding more). Food that the worms like include:

- Banana skins and other fruit like apples

- Carrot peels

- Egg shells

- A very small amount of coffee grounds

- Tea leaves

Do NOT feed the worms the following:

- Orange peels or other citrus scraps (these are toxic to worms)

- Meat

- Fish

- Dairy

- Junk food

The bins will sustain the worms for about a week. The worms will consume the newspaper and the paper towel within that time and should be either moved to a larger compost bin or students should empty their bins into a garden.

Mathematics Connection: Use the information teams found in their research in Lesson 2 about the capacity of various types of compost systems to calculate the size of compost system that would be required for school lunch food waste. This will require estimating how many pounds of compostable food waste students will dispose of per week. To make this estimate, you may wish to use the school lunch waste findings from Lesson 1 or you may wish to use an estimate provided by the school's cafeteria or maintenance staff.

ELA Connection: Have students make a plan for disseminating the composting campaign materials they created to make them available to the school community. This may include duplicating brochures and flyers, arranging for space to hang posters, making announcements on the school's public address system, or making presentations to other classes in the school.

Social Studies Connection: Not applicable

Evaluation/Assessment

Students may be assessed on the following performance tasks and other measures listed.

Performance Tasks

- Measure It diagrams
- Composting system prototypes/models (see rubric in Appendix A)
- Prototype It graphic organizers
- Composting system presentations (see rubric in Appendix A)
- Composting system budgets
- Composting publicity campaign materials

Other Measures

- Teacher observations
- STEM Research Notebook entries
- Student participation in teams

INTERNET RESOURCES

"How to Use Compost" video

- *www.youtube.com/watch?v=NpdoftbXPVk*

"Urban Farms" video

- *www.youtube.com/watch?v=qJAnBGHhjAc*

"Worms at Work: 20 Days Timelapse of Vermiposting" video

- *www.youtube.com/watch?v=n9Mnf9ysNSs*

"Worm Farm" video

- https://gpb.pbslearningmedia.org/resource/3daedfdc-edec-4c2e-b301-850cb5a8653e/3daedfdc-edec-4c2e-b301-850cb5a8653e/

Prototype It

Name:_____ Type of Compost System: _____

Plan. Use the diagram you created on graph paper to mark out the space for your composting system on the foam board provided (hint: you may want to cut the space out of your graph paper and trace it onto your foam board with pencil).

- What improvements could you make on the examples of the composting system you found while doing your research? Be creative!

- What features will you include in your model? You must include a prototype of your composting system in the space you have designated; however, you may also include landscape features such as sidewalks, building walls, trees, grass, etc. Make a list of what you will include.

- What materials will you need to create your model? Look at the materials your teacher has on hand. Make a list of what you need.

- Make a sketch of your prototype system on the back of this sheet. Label the materials you will use.

- How will you divide the work of building your prototype among team members?

Try. Gather your supplies and begin to build your model!

Test. Ask for feedback from another team. Do they have any suggestions?

Decide. Based on the feedback you received, will you change anything?

Share. You will present your prototype composting system to the class. Be sure to point out its features and why this system would be useful for the school.

Composting System Budget
Student Handout

Name:_____

Expenses			
Type of Material	Unit Cost	Amount Needed	Total Cost (Unit Cost ×Amount Needed)
Total Expenses			

Income and Donations	
Type of Income or Value of Donation	Amount of Income or Value of Donation
Total Income and Value of Donations	

Total Expenses – Total Income and Value of Donations =_____

If this number is less than zero, you will need to find more income or donations. If it is greater than zero, you have more than enough money to create your system.

Lesson Plan 4:
The Compost System Design Challenge

Students will address the optional component of the module challenge in this lesson by creating a full-scale composting system for school use. Students will also create a plan to maintain the compost and to collect data about the compost over time. Student teams will conduct research on topics to create a troubleshooting guide for the compost system as part of an ongoing maintenance plan. The class will make a decision about how the compost will be used, and will launch their publicity campaign in the school.

ESSENTIAL QUESTIONS

- How can we build a full-size compost system?

- What do we need to do to maintain our compost system?

- How will we use our compost?

ESTABLISHED GOALS AND OBJECTIVES

At the conclusion of this lesson, students will be able to do the following:

- Apply their understanding of composting principles and composting systems to create a full-scale composting system for school use

- Explain how to maintain and sustain the compost systems

- Identify data that can be collected about compost and create a plan to collect those data

- Identify potential problems that may arise in a composting system and identify solutions for those problems

- Explain how compost is used in gardening

TIME REQUIRED

5 days (approximately 30 minutes each day; see Table 3.10, p. 39).

MATERIALS

Required Materials for Lesson 4

- STEM Research Notebooks

- Computer with Internet access for viewing videos

- Chart paper

- Markers

- Materials for composting systems (these will vary depending on what type(s) of systems you will build, what designs you choose to use, and the size of the unit you build). Basic lists are included below:

Wire-Mesh Holding Unit

- o   Mesh screen
- o   Scrap wood
- o   Basic hand tools (for example, hammer, screwdriver, hand saw, pliers, measuring tape, flexible metal ruler, framing square, etc.)
- o   Sawhorse
- o   Long straight-edge or chalk snap line
- o   Heavy-duty wire or tin snips
- o   Metal file (for mesh screen bin)
- o   Staple gun
- o   Eye and ear protection
- o   Work gloves

Turning Unit

- o   Scrap wood
- o   Nails and/or screws
- o   Garbage can
- o   PVC pipe
- o   Basic hand tools (for example, hammer, screwdriver, hand saw, pliers, measuring tape, flexible metal ruler, framing square, etc.)
- o   Sawhorse
- o   Long straight-edge or chalk snap line
- o   Drill motor, drill paddle bit, and drill bits
- o   Hinges
- o   Latches
- o   Door handle
- o   "L" brackets
- o   Eye and ear protection
- o   Work gloves

Heap

- o   Scrap wood
- o   Nails and/or screws

- o Basic hand tools (for example, hammer, screwdriver, hand saw, pliers, measuring tape, flexible metal ruler, framing square, etc.)
- o Sawhorse
- o Long straight-edge or chalk snap line
- o Drill motor and drill bits
- o Eye and ear protection
- o Work gloves

Worm Compost Bin

- o Mesh screen
- o Scrap wood
- o Nails and/or screws
- o Hinges
- o One pound of worms for every 1/2 pound of food waste produced per day
- o Bedding for worms: peat moss, brown leaves, moistened, shredded newspaper or moistened, shredded cardboard
- o Basic hand tools (for example, hammer, screwdriver, hand saw, pliers, measuring tape, flexible metal ruler, framing square, etc.)
- o Sawhorse
- o Long straight-edge or chalk snap line
- o Drill motor and drill bits
- o Eye and ear protection
- o Work gloves

SAFETY NOTES

1. Remind students that personal protective equipment (safety glasses or goggles, aprons, and gloves) must be worn during the setup, hands-on, and take-down segments of activities.

2. Caution students not to eat any materials used in activities.

3. Students should use caution when handling scissors as the sharp points and blades can cut or puncture skin.

4. If students will be using a drill or other hand tools in this lesson, be sure to provide protective work gloves, demonstrate how the tool is used, and supervise students closely.

5. Tell students to be careful when handling containers. Cans and cut plastic may have sharp edges, which can cut or puncture skin. Glass or plastic bottles can break and cut skin.

6. Instruct students to be aware of and avoid poisonous plants and insects, any refuse, sharps (broken glass), and other hazards when they are outdoors.

7. Immediately wipe up any spilled water or soil on the floor to avoid a slip-and-fall hazard.

8. Have students wash hands with soap and water after activities are completed.

CONTENT STANDARDS AND KEY VOCABULARY

Table 4.10 lists the content standards from the *NGSS, CCSS,* and the Framework for 21st Century Learning that this lesson addresses, and Table 4.11 presents the key vocabulary. Vocabulary terms are provided for both teacher and student use. Teachers may choose to introduce some or all of the terms to students.

Table 4.10. Content Standards Addressed in STEM Road Map Module Lesson 4

NEXT GENERATION SCIENCE STANDARDS

PERFORMANCE OBJECTIVES
- 5-ESS2–1. Develop a model using an example to describe ways the geosphere, biosphere, hydrosphere, and/or atmosphere interact.
- 5-ESS3–1. Obtain and combine information about ways individual communities use science ideas to protect the Earth's resources and environment.
- 5-LSW-1. Develop a model to describe the movement of matter among plants, animals, decomposers, and the environment.
- 5-ETS1–2. Generate and compare multiple possible solutions to a problem based on how well each is likely to meet the criteria and constraints of the problem.
- 5-ETS1–3. Plan and carry out fair tests in which variables are controlled and failure points are considered to identify aspects of a model or prototype that can be improved.

DISCIPLINARY CORE IDEAS

ESS3.C: Human Impacts on Earth Systems
- Human activities in agriculture, industry, and everyday life have had major effects on the land, vegetation, streams, ocean, air, and even outer space. But individuals and communities are doing things to help protect Earth's resources and environment.

ETS1.A: Defining and Delimiting Engineering Problems
- Possible solutions to a problem are limited by available materials and resources (constraints). The success of a designed solution is determined by considering the desired features of a solution (criteria). Different proposals for solutions can be compared on the basis of how well each one meets the specified criteria for success or how well each takes the constraints into account.

CROSSCUTTING CONCEPTS

Systems and System Models
- A system is a group of related parts that make up a whole and can carry out functions its individual parts cannot.
- A system can be described in terms of its components and their interactions.

Cause and Effect
- Events have causes that generate observable patterns.
- Simple tests can be designed to gather evidence to support or refute student ideas about causes.

Influence of Science, Engineering, and Technology on Society and the Natural World
- People's needs and wants change over time, as do their demands for new and improved technologies.
- Engineers improve existing technologies or develop new ones to increase their benefits, decrease known risks, and meet societal demands.

SCIENCE AND ENGINEERING PRACTICES

Asking Questions and Defining Problems
- Ask questions about what would happen if a variable is changed.
- Identify scientific (testable) and non-scientific (non-testable) questions.
- Ask questions that can be investigated and predict reasonable outcomes based on patterns such as cause and effect relationships.
- Use prior knowledge to describe problems that can be solved.
- Define a simple design problem that can be solved through the development of an object, tool, process, or system and includes several criteria for success and constraints on materials, time, or cost.

Planning and Carrying Out Investigations
- Plan and conduct an investigation collaboratively to produce data to serve as the basis for evidence, using fair tests in which variables are controlled and the number of trials considered.
- Evaluate appropriate methods and/or tools for collecting data.
- Make observations and/or measurements to produce data to serve as the basis for evidence for an explanation of a phenomenon or test a design solution.
- Make predictions about what would happen if a variable changes.
- Test two different models of the same proposed object, tool, or process to determine which better meets criteria for success.

Constructing Explanations and Designing Solutions
- Construct an explanation of observed relationships (for example, the distribution of plants in the back yard).
- Use evidence (for example, measurements, observations, patterns) to construct or support an explanation or design a solution to a problem.

Continued

Table 4.10. (*continued*)

- Identify the evidence that supports particular points in an explanation.
- Apply scientific ideas to solve design problems.
- Generate and compare multiple solutions to a problem based on how well they meet the criteria and constraints of the design solution.

Obtaining, Evaluating, and Communicating Information
- Read and comprehend grade-appropriate complex texts and/or other reliable media to summarize and obtain scientific and technical ideas and describe how they are supported by evidence.
- Compare and/or combine across complex texts and/or other reliable media to support the engagement in other scientific and/or engineering practices.
- Combine information in written text with that contained in corresponding tables, diagrams, and/or charts to support the engagement in other scientific and/or engineering practices.
- Obtain and combine information from books and/or other reliable media to explain phenomena or solutions to a design problem.
- Communicate scientific and/or technical information orally and/or in written formats, including various forms of media as well as tables, diagrams, and charts

COMMON CORE STATE STANDARDS FOR MATHEMATICS

MATHEMATICAL PRACTICES
- 5.MP1. Make sense of problems and persevere in solving them.
- 5.MP2. Reason abstractly and quantitatively.
- 5.MP3. Construct viable arguments and critique the reasoning of others.
- 5.MP4. Model with mathematics.
- 5.MP5. Use appropriate tools strategically.
- 5.MP6. Attend to precision.
- 5.MP7. Look for and make use of structure.
- 5.MP8. Look for and express regularity in repeated reasoning.

MATHEMATICAL CONTENT
- MD.A.1. Convert among different-sized standard measurement units within a given measurement system (for example, convert 5 cm to 0.05 m), and use these conversions in solving multi-step, real world problems.
- MD.C.5. Relate volume to the operations of multiplication and addition and solve real world and mathematical problems involving volume.

COMMON CORE STATE STANDARDS FOR ENGLISH LANGUAGE ARTS

READING STANDARDS
- RI.5.1. Quote accurately from a text when explaining what the text says explicitly and when drawing inferences from the text.
- RI.5.3. Explain the relationships or interactions between two or more individuals, events, ideas, or concepts in a historical, scientific, or technical text based on specific information in the text.
- RI.5.4. Determine the meaning of general academic and domain-specific words and phrases in a text relevant to a grade 5 topic or subject area.

- RI.5.7. Draw on information from multiple print or digital sources, demonstrating the ability to locate an answer to a question quickly or to solve a problem efficiently.
- RI.5.9. Integrate information from several texts on the same topic in order to write or speak about the subject knowledgeably.

WRITING STANDARDS
- W.5.1. Write opinion pieces on topics or texts, supporting a point of view with reasons and information.
- W.5.2. Write informative/explanatory texts to examine a topic and convey ideas and information clearly.
- W.5.4. Produce clear and coherent writing in which the development and organization are appropriate to task, purpose, and audience.
- W.5.6. With some guidance and support from adults, use technology, including the Internet, to produce and publish writing as well as to interact and collaborate with others; demonstrate sufficient command of keyboarding skills to type a minimum of two pages in a single sitting.
- W.5.7. Conduct short research projects that use several sources to build knowledge through investigation of different aspects of a topic.
- W.5.8. Recall relevant information from experiences or gather relevant information from print and digital sources; summarize or paraphrase information in notes and finished work, and provide a list of sources.

SPEAKING AND LISTENING STANDARDS
- SL.5.1. Engage effectively in a range of collaborative discussions (one-on-one, in groups, and teacher-led) with diverse partners on grade 5 topics and texts, building on others' ideas and expressing their own clearly.
- SL.5.4. Report on a topic or text or present an opinion, sequencing ideas logically and using appropriate facts and relevant, descriptive details to support main ideas or themes; speak clearly at an understandable pace.
- SL.5.5. Include multimedia components (for example, graphics, sound) and visual displays in presentations when appropriate to enhance the development of main ideas or themes.
- SL.5.6. Adapt speech to a variety of contexts and tasks, using formal English when appropriate to task and situation.

FRAMEWORK FOR 21ST CENTURY LEARNING
Interdisciplinary themes (financial, economic, & business literacy; environmental literacy); Learning and Innovation Skills; Information, Media & Technology Skills; Life and Career Skills

Table 4.11. Key Vocabulary for Lesson 4

Key Vocabulary	Definition
data	a collection of information about something
troubleshooting	a way to solve problems that involves identifying the cause and identifying solutions

TEACHER BACKGROUND INFORMATION

If you have chosen to build a full-size composting system for the school, the class will build the school compost system during this lesson. The unit to be constructed will depend on the arrangements you have made with school administrators and staff. The class will make a decision about how the compost will be used, and will launch their publicity campaign in the school.

If the class is not constructing a full-size composting system at your school, you may wish to modify this lesson so that students create a proposal to the school or another institution about building a compost system as part of the composting publicity campaign. This proposal could include a class proposal about the type of system that could be built, the budget, instructions for building the system, the plan to maintain the compost, and the troubleshooting guide for the compost system.

The design of your compost system will vary according to your space and resource availability, school restrictions, and the food waste volume that you intend to accommodate (see Teacher Background Information in Lesson 1). General instructions for constructing the types of compost systems discussed in previous lessons (wire mesh holding unit, turning unit, heap, and worm bin) are provided below. Basic materials for each type of unit are provided in the Materials section of this lesson. You may wish to use alternative designs and/or work with local composting organizations and hardware suppliers to create plans for your systems. For more details on constructing various types of compost systems, see *www.lsuagcenter.com/portals/communications/publications/publications_catalog/lawn%20and%20garden/backyard%20composting.*

Wire-Mesh Holding Unit

Measure and cut a large rectangle of mesh screen to form the body of your wire-mesh holding unit. The height of the rectangle will be the height of your bin and the length of the rectangle will be the diameter of your bin. Using scrap wood, make four stakes that are longer than the height to put into the ground to maintain the shape of your wire bin. Staple the mesh screen to the stakes, making sure the top of the stake sticks out slightly above the top of the mesh screen. Roll the other side of the mesh screen up and over so that the unstaked end overlaps the staked end forming the shape of a cylinder and staple in place. Staple the remaining stakes around the mesh screen, secure into the ground, and begin using. File down any sharp edges.

Turning Unit

Drill holes in the center of the top and bottom of the garbage can as well as into the body of the garbage can for aeration. Measure, trace, and cut a door on the side of the garbage can and secure with L brackets. Place the PVC pipe through the center holes.

Make sure the pipe is long enough to protrude both ends. Build a wooden saw buck to hold the garbage can; nail two sets of scrap wood in an x-frame, and nail two pieces of scrap wood across the bottom for support. Set the garbage can with the pipe in the wooden saw buck.

Heap

Measure and cut four pieces of scrap wood into predetermined lengths. These will serve as the four corners to your square compost bin. Measure and cut 8–16 pieces of scrap wood into predetermined lengths to make up the walls of your compost bin. Ensure that there are spaces between the exterior boards to allow for aeration.

Worm Bin

Measure and cut four pieces of scrap wood into predetermined lengths. These will serve as the four corners to your square compost bin. Measure and cut 8–16 pieces of scrap wood into predetermined lengths to make up the walls of your compost bin. Build a cover made of mesh screen to ensure aeration. Secure the cover to the compost bin with hinges. Add water to dampen the bedding. Place the worms on top of the bedding.

Maintaining the Compost System

Once the compost unit is constructed, you will need to prepare the unit before adding food waste. For the wire mesh holding unit and heap, you will need to add "brown" materials such as sawdust, dried leaves, straw, and wood chips in thin layers between "green" materials (food waste, grass clippings). As a rule of thumb, you should maintain one part "green" matter to two parts "brown" matter. For the tumbler design, you should start with a small amount of existing compost, horse manure, or compost activator. For the worm bin, start by adding wet "brown" bedding materials (leaves, shredded paper, etc.), dry bedding materials, soil, and worms.

   The carbon to nitrogen (C:N) ratio is crucial to maintaining an effective compost system. A ratio of 25–30:1 is ideal. This ratio is affected by the amount of "browns" and "greens" in the system. As a general rule, "browns" are high in carbon while "greens" are high in nitrogen. Too much carbon in compost will cause decomposition to slow, while too much nitrogen will cause a foul odor. Sawdust and wood chips have some of the highest carbon content among the "browns" while garden waste and weeds have some of the highest nitrogen content among the "greens."

COMMON MISCONCEPTIONS

Since in this lesson students are synthesizing their learning from previous lessons to create compost systems, no new misconceptions are introduced. It will, however, be

helpful to review the misconceptions introduced in Lessons One to Three and be alert to ongoing misconceptions such as those presented.

PREPARATION FOR LESSON 4

Review the Teacher Background Information provided, make copies of the student handouts, assemble the materials for the lesson, and preview the videos recommended in the Learning Plan Components section below. You should be prepared to build the compost systems agreed upon by your school. It will be helpful to enlist the assistance of a carpenter, engineer, or other volunteers to assist in the building process. You may wish to ask volunteers to prepare materials in advance (for example, cut wood to length). Have all materials on hand and ensure that you have several class periods and access to workspace as you build your compost system.

Students will also launch their composting publicity campaign during this lesson. Make preparations for students to make announcements on the school's public address system or visit other classes in the school. You should also arrange for display and/or distribution of students' printed materials.

For the mathematics connection for this lesson, you should have available a blueprint or building plan that includes measurements. A sample blueprint image is provided at the end of this lesson.

LEARNING PLAN COMPONENTS
Introductory Activity/Engagement

Connection to the Challenge: Introduce the lesson by telling students that they will complete the Compost System Design Challenge during this lesson by constructing a full-size school composting system. Review the "Need to Know" chart students created in their STEM Research Notebooks during Lesson 1 and ensure that students have included all information they learned during the module. Students will collect additional information during this lesson as they create a maintenance schedule and troubleshooting guide for the compost system.

Science Class: Tell students that they will build the compost system during this lesson, and introduce to students the type of compost system your school has agreed to have your class build. Remind students that composting not only reduces the solid waste going to landfills, but is also useful for gardening. Ask students for their ideas about how they will know when compost is ready to use, creating a class list. Introduce the following guidelines about when compost is ready to use (from CommonGroundCompost. com at *https://commongroundcompost.com/what-is-compost/*):

- Compost will be dark in color and crumbly in texture.

- It will smell like earth (not like chemicals).

- You will not be able to recognize the materials you added (food waste) in the compost.

- The compost will be about half the size it was originally.

- The pile's temperature should be about the same as the air's temperature.

Ask students for their ideas about what they should do with the compost and how to use their compost, reminding students of the video "How to Use Compost" (*www. youtube.com/watch?v=NpdoftbXPVk*) they watched in the last lesson. Hold a class discussion about how to use the compost the class's composting system will create and how the compost will be delivered to its destination.

Mathematics Connection: Ask students to consider if construction workers and other building professionals like architects use mathematics. Show students a sample of a blueprint or a building plan and ask them to interpret what the numbers on the plan mean. Lead students to understand that people who work in building careers of any kind need to understand fractions and various measurement units, including the English and metric systems. Tell students that as they build their composting system they will need to measure and work with measurements and possibly fractions. Provide students with tape measures and have them measure a variety of objects and perform calculations with those measurements (for example, measure two sides of your desk and find the sum of the two sides; measure the height of your desk in both inches and centimeters; measure the length of the hallway in centimeters and convert it to meters).

Provide students with a series of mathematical problems related to construction. For example: Show students a piece of wood is 3 feet long, but tell them that for the compost bin you are building it needs to be cut to 1 foot 7¾ inches long. How much will they need to cut off?

ELA Connection and Social Studies Connections: Tell students that in this lesson they are going to present their composting publicity materials to the school community. Have students post materials in spots around the school and have students prepare for making announcements or presentations if they will do so.

Activity/Exploration

Science Class and Mathematics Connection: Continue having students make periodic observations of the four ecosystems created in Lesson One. Ask students to share what they noticed about the ecosystems – i.e., did they observe any change since their last observation or since the first day?

In this lesson, students will build their full-size compost system in the Build It activity.

Build It

The process used to build the compost system will depend on the variables discussed in the Teacher Background Information section (i.e., type and size of system); therefore, specific procedures are not provided. An overview of construction for each system is provided in the Teacher Background Information section of this lesson.

Once the compost unit is constructed, you will need to prepare the unit before adding food waste. For the wire mesh holding unit and heap, you will need to add "brown" materials such as sawdust, dried leaves, straw, and wood chips in thin layers between "green" materials (food waste, grass clippings). As a rule of thumb, you should maintain one part "green" matter to two parts "brown" matter. For the tumbler design, you should start with a small amount of existing compost, horse manure, or compost activator. For the worm bin, start by adding wet "brown" bedding materials (leaves, shredded paper, etc.), dry bedding materials, soil, and worms.

ELA and Social Studies Connection: Have students present their composting publicity materials to the school community.

Explanation

Science Class and Mathematics Connection: Students will create a maintenance schedule and data collection for the compost system.

Maintenance Schedule and Data Collection

Students should work as a class to determine what sort of maintenance their compost system requires. Teams should have collected this information during their research in Lesson 2. Some types of compost systems require turning (wire-mesh holding unit, heap, and turning unit) on a regular basis. The compost system may also need to have water added periodically. Students should also consider how often they should remove compost, how and where it will be used, and who will do this. In addition, students should consider who will collect food scraps and add them to the compost system, and who will add additional "brown" material when necessary. As a class, create a maintenance calendar on which they record the maintenance needed and the individuals or teams responsible for that maintenance.

Collecting data about the compost system will also aid students in maintaining the compost system appropriately. Students should create charts in their STEM Research Notebooks on which they track data on a weekly basis. They should include factors such as observations of moisture level, odor, worm health (if worm composting was used), and measurements of temperature. A sample data collection chart is included at the end of this lesson.

ELA and Social Studies Connections: If students will be orally presenting their composting campaign materials to other students and/or school staff, review good presentation practices (for example, speaking in a clear voice, making eye contact, using language appropriate to the audience).

Remind students that composting is a type of recycling. Have students explore the interactive recycling game on the National Geographic Kids website: *https://kids.nation algeographic.com/games/action-adventure/article/recycle-roundup-new*. This game prompts students to clean up a park, sorting waste into trash, recycling, or compost.

Elaboration/Application of Knowledge

Science Class: Have students revisit the "Need to Know" chart they created during Lesson 1. Review the chart with students, asking whether they actually needed all the information they thought they needed, whether they were able to collect all the needed information, and whether there is anything else they would add to the chart now that they have constructed their compost system. Next, tell students that in order to best maintain their composting system they should be prepared for problems that might arise such as the compost developing a bad odor or attracting animals or insects. In order to do this, tell students that they will anticipate what problems might arise and be prepared with solutions for them by creating a troubleshooting guide.

Troubleshooting Guide

Students will create a troubleshooting guide that will provide information for individuals maintaining the system. Have each team of students address one of the following topics and conduct research:

- Odor

- Food not decomposing

- System attracting animals and/or flies

- Compost is not heating up

Students should identify the cause and solution for each problem and provide additional resources (for example, Internet links or books) using the Troubleshooting Guide student handout. Teams should each present their findings to the class. Combine teams' findings to create a comprehensive troubleshooting guide to provide to all individuals involved with the care and maintenance of the compost system.

Mathematics Connection: Not applicable

ELA and Social Studies Connection: Have students share their composting campaign materials with a wider audience (for example at a PTA meeting or at a town/city government meeting).

Evaluation/Assessment

Students may be assessed on the following performance tasks and other measures listed.

Performance Tasks

- Class composting system
- Maintenance schedule
- Data collection plan
- Troubleshooting guide

Other Measures

- Teacher observations
- STEM Research Notebook entries
- Student participation in teams

INTERNET RESOURCES

Resources for constructing various types of compost systems

- *www.lsuagcenter.com/portals/communications/publications/publications_catalog/lawn%20and%20garden/backyard%20composting*

Guidelines to identify finished compost

- *https://commongroundcompost.com/what-is-compost/*

"How to Use Compost" video

- *www.youtube.com/watch?v=NpdoftbXPVk*

Interactive recycling game

- *https://kids.nationalgeographic.com/games/action-adventure/article/recycle-roundup-new*

4

School Composting System
Sample Data Chart

Date	Moist to Touch? (yes or no)	Water Added (yes or no)	Odor (slight, moderate, strong)	Worm Health (moist and active, dry and inactive, etc.)	Food Decomposing (no, yes)	Temperature	Evidence of Animals

Troubleshooting Guide
Team Handout

Names:_____   _____

_____

The problem we researched was _____

Cause(s)	Solution(s)	Additional Resources

Sample Blueprint Image

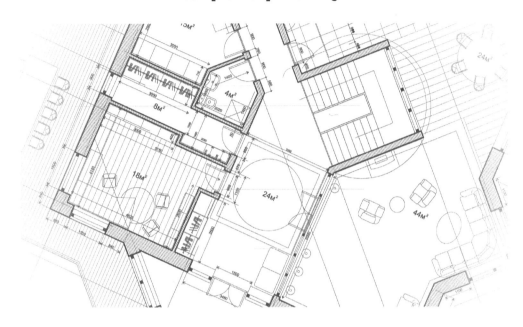

SUGGESTED BOOKS

Bowden, R. (2004). *Sustainable world: Waste*. KidHaven Press.

Brunner-Jass, R. (2013). *Stir it up: Mixing decimals*. Norwood House Press.

Dixon, N. (2005). *Lowdown on earthworms*. Fitzhenry & Whiteside.

Glaser, L. (2010). *Garbage helps our compost system grow: A compost story*. Millbrook Press.

Hanson-Harding, B. (2014). *Composting: Turn food waste into rich soil*. Rosen Publishing.

Hoe, S. (2009). *Maps and mapping: Habitats*. Gareth Stevens Publishing.

Katz-Cooper, S. (2010). *The compost heap* (Horrible Habitats Series). Raintree.

Koontz, R. (2006). *Composting: Nature's recyclers*. Picture Window Books.

Lay, R. (2013). *A green kid's guide to composting*. ABDO Publishing Group.

Linde, B. (2005). *Climates of the world*. Rosen Publishing.

Nadeau, I. (2006). *Interdependence of organisms and the environment*. PowerKids Press.

Parker, S. (2006). *Microlife that rots things*. Raintree.

Pascoe, E. (2003). *The ecosystem of a fallen tree*. Rosen Publishing.

Pipe, J. (2008). *Earth's ecosystems*. Gareth Stevens Publishing.

Porter, E. (2013). *What's sprouting in my trash?* Capstone Press.

Schuh, M., & Saunders-Smith, G. (2012). *Compost basics*. Capstone Press.

Siddals, M. (2010). *Compost stew: An A to Z recipe for the Earth*. Crown Publishing.

Stwertka, E., & Stwertka, A. (1993). *Cleaning up: How trash becomes treasure*. Simon & Schuster.

Winter, J. (2010). *Here comes the garbage barge!* Random House Children's Books.

Zoehffld, K. (2012). *Secrets of the compost system: Food chains and the food web in our backyard*. Alfred Knopf.

REFERENCES

Coughlin, P. (n.d.). *School composting: A manual for Connecticut schools*. State of Connecticut Department of Environmental Protection. *https://portal.ct.gov/-/media/DEEP/compost/compost_pdf/schmanualpdf.pdf*

TRANSFORMING LEARNING WITH COMPOSTING AND THE *STEM ROAD MAP CURRICULUM SERIES*

Carla C. Johnson

This chapter serves as a conclusion to the **Composting** integrated STEM curriculum module, but it is just the beginning of the transformation of your classroom that is possible through use of the *STEM Road Map Curriculum Series.* In this book, many key resources have been provided to make learning meaningful for your students through integration of science, technology, engineering, and mathematics, as well as social studies and English language arts, into powerful problem- and project-based instruction. First, the **Composting** curriculum is grounded in the latest theory of learning for students in **grade 5** specifically. Second, as your students work through this module, they engage in using the engineering design process (EDP) and build prototypes like engineers and STEM professionals in the real world. Third, students acquire important knowledge and skills grounded in national academic standards in mathematics, English language arts, science, and 21st century skills that will enable their learning to be deeper, retained longer, and applied throughout, illustrating the critical connections within and across disciplines. Finally, authentic formative assessments, including strategies for differentiation and addressing misconceptions, are embedded within the curriculum activities.

The **Composting** curriculum in the **Sustainable Systems** STEM Road Map theme can be used in single-content classrooms (e.g., mathematics) where there is only one teacher or expanded to include multiple teachers and content areas across classrooms. Through the exploration of the **Composting** lesson plans, students engage in a real-world STEM problem on the first day of instruction and gather necessary knowledge and skills along the way in the context of solving the problem.

The other topics in the *STEM Road Map Curriculum Series* are designed in a similar manner, and NSTA Press and Routledge have published additional volumes in this series for this and other grade levels, and have plans to publish more.

DOI: 10.4324/9781003370772-7

For an up-to-date list of volumes in the series, please visit *www.routledge.com/ STEM-Road-Map-Curriculum-Series/book-series/SRM* (for titles co-published by Routledge and NSTA Press), or *www.nsta.org/book-series/stem-road-map-curriculum* (for titles published by NSTA Press).

If you are interested in professional development opportunities focused on the STEM Road Map specifically or integrated STEM or STEM programs and schools over-all, contact the lead editor of this project, Dr. Carla C. Johnson, Professor of Science Education at NC State University. Someone from the team will be in touch to design a program that will meet your individual, school, or district needs.

APPENDIX A

RUBRICS

PRESENTATION RUBRIC page 1 of 2

Team Name:

	Below Standard (0–2)	Approaching Standard (3–4)	Meets or Exceeds Standard (5–6)	Team Score
	• Team includes little interesting and factual information and may omit important information. • Presentation does not reflect understanding of key science and/or mathematics concepts relevant to the presentation topic.	• Team includes some interesting and factual information but could provide more details. • Presentation reflects some understanding of key science concepts and/or mathematics relevant to the presentation topic but may be incomplete or include some inaccuracies.	• Team includes complete, interesting, and factual information. • Presentation reflects understanding of all key science and/or mathematics concepts relevant to the presentation topic.	
	• Team does not have a main idea or organizational strategy. • Presentation does not include an introduction and/or conclusion. • Presentation is confusing and uninformative. • Team uses presentation time poorly and it is too short or too long.	• Team has a main idea and organizational strategy, although it may not be clear. • Presentation includes both or either an introduction and conclusion. • Presentation is fairly coherent, well organized, and informative. • Team uses presentation time adequately, but presentation may be slightly too short or too long.	• Team has a clear main idea and organizational strategy. • Presentation includes both an introduction and conclusion. • Presentation is coherent, well organized, and informative. • Team uses presentation time well and presentation is an appropriate length.	
	• Only one or two team members participate in the presentation. • Presenters are difficult to understand. • Presenters use language inappropriate for audience (slang, poor grammar, frequent filler words such as "uh," "um").	• Some, but not all, team members participate in the presentation. • Most presenters are understandable, but volume may be too low or some presenters may mumble. • Presenters use some language inappropriate for audience (slang, poor grammar, some use of filler words such as "uh," "um").	• All team members participate in the presentation. • Presenters are easy to understand. • Presenters use appropriate language for audience (no slang or poor grammar, infrequent use of filler words such as "uh," "um").	

PRESENTATION RUBRIC page 2 of 2

• Team does not use any visual aids to presentation. • Visual aids are used but do not add to the presentation.	• Team uses some visual aids to presentation, but they may be poorly executed or distract from the presentation.	• Team uses well-produced visual aids or media that clarifies and enhances presentation.
• Team fails to respond to questions from audience or responds inappropriately.	• Team responds appropriately to audience questions but responses may be brief, incomplete, or unclear.	• Team responds clearly and in detail to audience questions and seeks clarification of questions.

TOTAL SCORE:

COMMENTS:

CREATIVE WRITING RUBRIC page 1 of 2

Name: _____

Categories (Components)	Missing or Unrelated (0 points)	Beginning (1 point)	Developing (2 points)	Meets Expectations (3 points)	Exceeds Expectations (4 points)	Score
Story Structure	Component is missing or unrelated.	The story has little structure and two out of the three components (beginning, middle, or end) are missing or are not related to the story's topic.	The story is missing one component of structure (beginning, middle, or end) or the components are not related to the story's topic.	The story has a beginning, middle, and end that relate to the story's topic.	The story has a clearly presented beginning, middle, and end that focus on the story's topic.	
Story Elements	Component is missing or unrelated.	No problem is presented. Characters are not used or they are difficult to identify. No clear solution is presented.	The problem may be confusing and the setting vague. Characters may not be introduced or identified or there may be no solution.	The problem is stated clearly and presented in a specific setting. Characters are identified, and a solution is presented.	The problem is clearly and creatively presented in a specific and well-described setting. Characters are well developed and a solution develops from the interaction of the story elements.	

CREATIVE WRITING RUBRIC page 2 of 2

Sentence Structure and Description	Sentence structure interferes with reader's ability to understand the story and no details are included. Dialogue is not used.	Sentence structure interferes with the flow of the story and no details are included. Dialogue is not used.	Sentence structure is repetitive and may interfere with the flow of the story. Few details are used. Dialogue is not used appropriately.	Sentences are structured correctly with some variety. Sentences contribute to the flow of the story and contain some description. Dialogue is used appropriately.	Sentence structure is clear and easy to understand and contributes to the flow of the story. Sentences use engaging description to enhance the story. Dialogue is used appropriately and enhances the story.
Grammar and Spelling	Most punctuation marks are missing and most words are spelled incorrectly.	Few punctuation marks are used, and many words are spelled incorrectly.	Punctuation is used incorrectly and there are spelling errors.	Proper punctuation and spelling are used in most places with a few errors.	Writing demonstrates a strong grasp of proper punctuation and spelling, and there are few or no errors.

TOTAL SCORE:

COMMENTS:

PROTOTYPE DESIGN RUBRIC

Team Name: _____

Team Performance	Below Standard (0–1)	Approaching Standard (2–3)	Meets or Exceeds Standard (4–5)	Team Score
Creativity and Innovation	• Design reflects little creativity with use of materials, lack of understanding of project purpose, and no innovative design features. • Design is impractical. • Design has several elements that do not fit.	• Design reflects some creativity with use of materials, a basic understanding of project purpose, and limited innovative design features. • Design is limited in practicality. • Design has some interesting elements, but may be excessive or inappropriate.	• Design reflects creative use of materials, a sound understanding of project purpose, and distinct innovative design features. • Design is practical. • Design is well-crafted, includes interesting elements that are appropriate for the purpose.	
Conceptual Understanding	• Design incorporates no or few features that reflect conceptual understanding of concepts.	• Design incorporates some features that reflect a limited conceptual understanding of concepts.	• Design incorporates several features that reflect a sound conceptual understanding of concepts.	
TOTAL SCORE:				
COMMENTS:				

WRITING RUBRIC – INFORMATIVE TEXT

Team Name: _____

	Below Standard (0–1)	Approaching Standard (2–3)	Meets Standard (4–5)
Content	Does not include all required information. Few facts, details, and examples are included.	Most information is provided, but some information is missing or inaccurate. Some facts, details, and examples are included.	All information is provided and is accurate. Relevant and interesting facts, details, and examples are included.
Organization	Organization is not clear. No introduction and/or conclusion is included. Information may be grouped in a confusing manner and/or paragraph structure is weak.	An organizational structure is evident. Information is grouped appropriately for the most part; however, paragraph structure may be weak or some information may be grouped inappropriately.	A clear organizational structure is evident. All information is grouped appropriately and paragraphs are structured appropriately.
Focus	The writer's focus is unclear or incoherent. There may be inappropriate or irrelevant information included. Content vocabulary is not used consistently or used inappropriately.	The writer's focus is clear; however, there may be some unnecessary or confusing information included. Content vocabulary is used appropriately.	The writer's focus is clear and all information provided is relevant to the topic. Content vocabulary is used appropriately.
Language and usage	The writer makes consistent errors in the conventions of standard English grammar (for example, verb tenses, capitalization, punctuation) and spelling.	There are few errors in the conventions of standard English grammar (for example, verb tenses, capitalization, punctuation) and spelling.	The writer demonstrates a firm grasp of conventions of standard English grammar (for example, verb tenses, capitalization, punctuation) and spelling.
TOTAL SCORE:			
COMMENTS:			

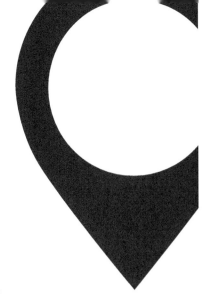

APPENDIX B

CONTENT STANDARDS ADDRESSED
IN THIS MODULE

NEXT GENERATION SCIENCE STANDARDS

Table B1 lists the science and engineering practices, disciplinary core ideas, and cross-cutting concepts this module addresses. The supported performance expectations are as follows:

- 5-ESS2-1. Develop a model using an example to describe ways the geosphere, biosphere, hydrosphere, and/or atmosphere interact.

- 5-ESS3-1. Obtain and combine information about ways individual communities use science ideas to protect the Earth's resources and environment.

- 5-LSW-1. Develop a model to describe the movement of matter among plants, animals, decomposers, and the environment.

- 5-ETS1-2. Generate and compare multiple possible solutions to a problem based on how well each is likely to meet the criteria and constraints of the problem.

- 5-ETS1-3. Plan and carry out fair tests in which variables are controlled and failure points are considered to identify aspects of a model or prototype that can be improved.

Table B.1. Next Generation Science Standards (NGSS)

SCIENCE AND ENGINEERING PRACTICES

ASKING QUESTIONS AND DEFINING PROBLEMS

- Ask questions about what would happen if a variable is changed.
- Identify scientific (testable) and non-scientific (non-testable) questions.
- Ask questions that can be investigated and predict reasonable outcomes based on patterns such as cause and effect relationships.
- Use prior knowledge to describe problems that can be solved.
- Define a simple design problem that can be solved through the development of an object, tool, process, or system and includes several criteria for success and constraints on materials, time, or cost.

PLANNING AND CARRYING OUT INVESTIGATIONS

- Plan and conduct an investigation collaboratively to produce data to serve as the basis for evidence, using fair tests in which variables are controlled and the number of trials considered.
- Evaluate appropriate methods and/or tools for collecting data.
- Make observations and/or measurements to produce data to serve as the basis for evidence for an explanation of a phenomenon or test a design solution.
- Make predictions about what would happen if a variable changes.
- Test two different models of the same proposed object, tool, or process to determine which better meets criteria for success.

CONSTRUCTING EXPLANATIONS AND DESIGNING SOLUTIONS

- Construct an explanation of observed relationships (e.g., the distribution of plants in the back yard).
- Use evidence (e.g., measurements, observations, patterns) to construct or support an explanation or design a solution to a problem.
- Identify the evidence that supports particular points in an explanation.
- Apply scientific ideas to solve design problems.
- Generate and compare multiple solutions to a problem based on how well they meet the criteria and constraints of the design solution.

OBTAINING, EVALUATING, AND COMMUNICATING INFORMATION

- Read and comprehend grade-appropriate complex texts and/or other reliable media to summarize and obtain scientific and technical ideas and describe how they are supported by evidence.
- Compare and/or combine across complex texts and/or other reliable media to support the engagement in other scientific and/or engineering practices.
- Combine information in written text with that contained in corresponding tables, diagrams, and/or charts to support the engagement in other scientific and/or engineering practices.
- Obtain and combine information from books and/or other reliable media to explain phenomena or solutions to a design problem.
- Communicate scientific and/or technical information orally and/or in written formats, including various forms of media as well as tables, diagrams, and charts.

DISCIPLINARY CORE IDEAS

ESS3.C: HUMAN IMPACTS ON EARTH SYSTEMS

- Human activities in agriculture, industry, and everyday life have had major effects on the land, vegetation, streams, ocean, air, and even outer space. But individuals and communities are doing things to help protect Earth's resources and environment.

ETS1.A: DEFINING AND DELIMITING ENGINEERING PROBLEMS

- Possible solutions to a problem are limited by available materials and resources (constraints). The success of a designed solution is determined by considering the desired features of a solution (criteria). Different proposals for solutions can be compared on the basis of how well each one meets the specified criteria for success or how well each takes the constraints into account.

ETS1.B: DEVELOPING POSSIBLE SOLUTIONS

- Research on a problem should be carried out before beginning to design a solution. Testing a solution involves investigating how well it performs under a range of likely conditions.
- At whatever stage, communicating with peers about proposed solutions is an important part of the design process, and shared ideas can lead to improved designs.
- Tests are often designed to identify failure points or difficulties, which suggest the elements of the design that need to be improved.

ETS1.C: OPTIMIZING THE DESIGN SOLUTION

- Different solutions need to be tested in order to determine which of them best solves the problem, given the criteria and the constraints.

CROSSCUTTING CONCEPTS

SYSTEMS AND SYSTEM MODELS

- A system can be described in terms of its components and their interactions.

CAUSE AND EFFECT

- Events have causes that generate observable patterns.
- Simple tests can be designed to gather evidence to support or refute student ideas about causes.

INFLUENCE OF SCIENCE, ENGINEERING, AND TECHNOLOGY ON SOCIETY AND THE NATURAL WORLD

- People's needs and wants change over time, as do their demands for new and improved technologies.
- Engineers improve existing technologies or develop new ones to increase their benefits, decrease known risks, and meet societal demands.

Source: NGSS Lead States. (2013). *Next Generation Science Standards: For states, by states.* National Academies Press. *www.nextgenscience.org/next-generation-science-standards.*

Table B.2. Common Core Mathematics and English/Language Arts (ELA) Standards

Common Core State Mathematics Standards	Common Core State English Language Arts (ELA)
MATHEMATICAL PRACTICES • MP1. Make sense of problems and persevere in solving them. • MP2. Reason abstractly and quantitatively. • MP3. Construct viable arguments and critique the reasoning of others. • MP4. Model with mathematics. • MP5. Use appropriate tools strategically. • MP6. Attend to precision. • MP7. Look for and make use of structure. • MP8. Look for and express regularity in repeated reasoning. **MATHEMATICAL CONTENT** • MD.A.1. Convert among different-sized standard measurement units within a given measurement system (e.g., convert 5 cm to 0.05 m), and use these conversions in solving multi-step, real world problems. • MD.B2. Make a line plot to display a data set of measurements in fractions of a unit (1/2, 1/4, 1/8). Use operations on fractions for this grade to solve problems involving information presented in line plots. • MD.C.5. Relate volume to the operations of multiplication and addition and solve real world and mathematical problems involving volume.	**READING STANDARDS** • RI.5.1. Quote accurately from a text when explaining what the text says explicitly and when drawing inferences from the text. • RI.5.3. Explain the relationships or interactions between two or more individuals, events, ideas, or concepts in a historical, scientific, or technical text based on specific information in the text. • RI.5.4. Determine the meaning of general academic and domain-specific words and phrases in a text relevant to *a grade 5 topic or subject area.* • RI.5.7. Draw on information from multiple print or digital sources, demonstrating the ability to locate an answer to a question quickly or to solve a problem efficiently. • RI.5.9. Integrate information from several texts on the same topic in order to write or speak about the subject knowledgeably. **WRITING STANDARDS** • W.5.1. Write opinion pieces on topics or texts, supporting a point of view with reasons and information. • W.5.2. Write informative/explanatory texts to examine a topic and convey ideas and information clearly. • W.5.4. Produce clear and coherent writing in which the development and organization are appropriate to task, purpose, and audience. • W.5.6. With some guidance and support from adults, use technology, including the Internet, to produce and publish writing as well as to interact and collaborate with others; demonstrate sufficient command of keyboarding skills to type a minimum of two pages in a single sitting. • W.5.7. Conduct short research projects that use several sources to build knowledge through investigation of different aspects of a topic. • W.5.8. Recall relevant information from experiences or gather relevant information from print and digital sources; summarize or paraphrase information in notes and finished work, and provide a list of sources.

Table B.2. (*continued*)

Common Core State Mathematics Standards	Common Core State English Language Arts (ELA)
	SPEAKING AND LISTENING STANDARDS • SL.5.1. Engage effectively in a range of collaborative discussions (one-on-one, in groups, and teacher-led) with diverse partners on *grade 5 topics and texts*, building on others' ideas and expressing their own clearly. • SL.5.4. Report on a topic or text or present an opinion, sequencing ideas logically and using appropriate facts and relevant, descriptive details to support main ideas or themes; speak clearly at an understandable pace. • SL.5.5. Include multimedia components (for example, graphics, sound) and visual displays in presentations when appropriate to enhance the development of main ideas or themes. • SL.5.6. Adapt speech to a variety of contexts and tasks, using formal English when appropriate to task and situation.

Source: National Governors Association Center for Best Practices and Council of Chief State School Officers (NGAC and CCSSO). (2010). *Common core state standards.* NGAC and CCSSO.

Table B.3. 21st Century Skills from the Framework for 21st Century Learning

21st Century Skills	Learning Skills and Technology Tools	Teaching Strategies	Evidence of Success
Interdisciplinary Themes	• Global Awareness • Economic, Business, and Entrepreneurial Literacy • Health Literacy • Environmental Literacy	• Facilitate student use of the engineering design process (EDP) to create composting system prototypes and a full-scale composting system. • Facilitate the creation of a budget for the creation of full-scale composting systems. • Students observe changes in the ecosystems. • Provide opportunities for students to consider how to reduce solid waste in landfills.	• Students demonstrate an understanding of the EDP and use it successfully to create composting system prototypes and a full-scale composting system. • Students create a balanced budget for a full-scale composting system, identifying expenses and sources of income. • Students track changes in the ecosystems and explore the interdependent relationships in ecosystems and the significant role decomposers play within these ecosystems.

Continued

Composting, Grade 5

Table B.3. (*continued*)

21st Century Skills	Learning Skills and Technology Tools	Teaching Strategies	Evidence of Success
Learning and Innovation Skills	• Creativity and Innovation • Critical Thinking and Problem Solving • Communication and Collaboration	• Introduce the EDP as a problem-solving framework. • Facilitate critical thinking and problem-solving skills through the design and building of composting system prototypes and a full-scale composting system. • Facilitate critical thinking and problem solving in the maintenance of classroom ecosystems and the full-scale composting system. • Provide examples of publicity materials for recycling and composting systems as examples for students' composting campaign. • Provide examples of fictional literature, emphasizing story structure, dialogue, and use of illustrations.	• Students demonstrate an understanding of the EDP through teamwork to design compost system prototypes. • Students demonstrate creativity and innovation, critical thinking and problem solving, communication, and collaboration as they plan, build, and maintain a full-scale composting system that utilizes their understanding of the interdependent relationships in ecosystems and the significant role decomposers play within these ecosystems. • Students create materials for a publicity campaign to promote composting. • Students create their own works of fiction.
Information, Media and Technology Skills	• Information Literacy • Media Literacy • Information Communication and Technology Literacy	• Engage students in guided practice and scaffolding strategies through the use of developmentally appropriate books, videos, and websites to advance their knowledge.	• Students acquire and use deeper content knowledge via information, media, and technology skills as they create compost system prototypes and plan and build a full-scale composting system.
Life and Career Skills	• Flexibility and Adaptability • Initiative and Self-Direction • Social and Cross-Cultural Skills • Productivity and Accountability • Leadership and Responsibility	• Facilitate student collaborative group work to foster life and career skills.	• Throughout this module, students collaborate to conduct research, complete design projects, and create a full-scale composting system.

Source: Partnership for 21st Century Learning. (2015). Framework for 21st Century Learning. *www.p21.org/our-work/ p21-framework.*

Table B.4. English Language Development Standards Addressed in STEM Road Map Module

English Language Development Standards: Grades 3–5 (WIDA, 2020)
ELD Standard 1: Social and Instructional Language
Multilingual learners narrate, inform, explain, and argue.
ELD Standard 2: Language for Language Arts
Multilingual learners will construct and interpret language arts narratives and arguments and construct and interpret informational texts.
ELD Standard 3: Language for Mathematics
Multilingual learners will interpret and construct mathematical explanations and arguments.
ELD Standard 4: Language for Science
Multilingual learners will interpret and construct scientific explanations and arguments.
ELD Standard 5: Language for Social Studies
Multilingual learners will interpret and construct social studies arguments.

Source: WIDA. (2020). *WIDA English language development standards framework, 2020 edition: Kindergarten–grade 12.* Board of Regents of the University of Wisconsin System. *https://wida.wisc.edu/sites/default/files/resource/WIDA-ELD-Standards-Framework-2020.pdf*

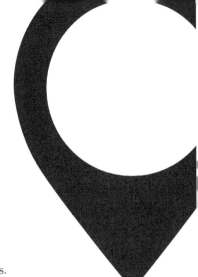

INDEX

Note: Page numbers in *italic* refer to figures and page numbers in **bold** refer to tables.

A

academic standards 1, 2, 145

Activity/Exploration phase 12, 18, 55–61, 87–91, 118–121, 137–138

animals in the classroom, responsible use of live 49

Appendix A 148–153

Appendix B 155–161

Application of Knowledge/Elaboration phase 12, 18, 62–63, 92–93, 121–124, 139

assessment 30; comprehensive system 14; formative 14–15; plan overview **33**; role of 13–14; summative 14, 15, 16

Assessment/Evaluation phase 12, 18, 63, 93–94, 124, 140

assessment maps 15–16, **33–36**

assignments, tiered 31

B

Background Information, Teacher 48–51, 83–84, 114–115, 134–135

blueprints: assessment maps 15–16, **33–36**; building plans 136, 137, 143

Brown, A., Moore, T.S. and Guzey, S.S. 6

Build It 138

C

career connections 49–50

cause and effect concept 3

community resources 40

compacting 30–31

complex problems 5

Compost System Design Challenge 24, 127–143

Composting Containers 90–91, 102–106

Composting Systems 76–106; Prototyping 107–126

content-focused formative assessments 15

contexts, varied environmental learning 31

Council of State Science Supervisors (CSSS) 19

creative writing rubric 150–151

criteria and constraints, problem 10–11

crosscutting concepts **45, 80, 111, 131**

curriculum 1, 2, 6, 7, 9

curriculum maps 2

cyclical learning process 16, *16*

D

deliverables **33**

desired outcomes 32, **32**

differentiation strategies 26, **26–27**, 30–31

E

Ecosystem Engineers 57–60, 67–74

Ecosystem Explorers 41–75

Ecosystem Showcase 61–63, 75

ecosystems 4

Elaboration/Application of Knowledge phase 12, 18, 62–63, 92–93, 121–124, 139

Engagement/Introductory Activity phase 12, 17, 53–55, 85–86, 117–118, 136–137

engineering design process (EDP) 9–11, *10*, 50–51, *65*, 86, 114, 117, 119, 120

English Language Arts (ELA): *Common Core State Standards* 2, 15, **46–47, 81–82, 113–114, 132–133, 158–159**; connections 55, 60, 62, 63, 90–91, 92, 93, 118, 120–121, 121, 124, 137, 138, 138–139, 139; prerequisite skills, knowledge application and differentiation strategies **27** *see also* Reading Standards; Speaking and Listening Standards; Writing Standards

English language development (ELD) standards **161**

English language learners, strategies for 31

NATIONAL SCIENCE TEACHING ASSOCIATION

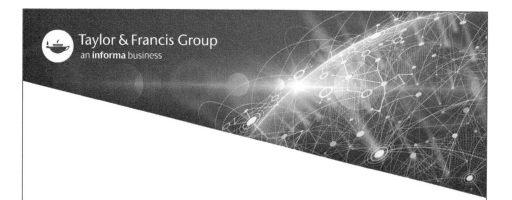

For Product Safety Concerns and Information please contact our
EU representative GPSR@taylorandfrancis.com Taylor & Francis
Verlag GmbH, Kaufingerstraße 24, 80331 München, Germany